Connecticut Icons

50 Symbols of the Nutmeg State

CHARLES MONAGAN

EDITOR OF **CONNECTICUT** MAGAZINE

INSIDERS' GUIDE®

GUILFORD, CONNECTICUT
AN IMPRINT OF THE GLOBE PEQUOT PRESS

INSIDERS' GUIDE®

All stories in this book appeared in slightly different form in *Connecticut Magazine*. They are used with permission. Photo credits appear on page iv.

Text design: Lisa Reneson

Library of Congress Cataloging-in-Publication Data is available.

ISBN-13: 978-0-7627-3548-8
ISBN-10: 0-7627-3548-1

Manufactured in China
First Edition/First Printing

In memory of my father, John S. Monagan,
who loved Connecticut and encouraged me to do the same.

Photo Credits

Pp. 1 and 63 courtesy of Devin Janosov; p. 2 © www.johnmcolumbus.com; p. 3 © Peter Sispoidis; p. 5 © 2006 Jack McConnell; p. 7 courtesy of the Peabody Museum; p. 9 courtesy of the Danbury Museum and Historical Society; p. 11 © Robert Levin; p. 13 © 2006 Jack McConnell; p. 15 courtesy of Douglas Foulke; p. 17 © Connecticut River Museum; p. 19 courtesy of Colt® (Colt® is a registered trademark of New Colt Holding Corp. All rights reserved. Used with permission.); p. 21 courtesy of M. J. Fiedler; p. 23 © Peter Sispoidis; p. 25 courtesy of The National Trust for Historic Preservation; p. 27 courtesy of Yale University; p. 29 © Jeff Kaufman; p. 31 © Robert Benson; p. 33 © 2004 The Wiffle Ball, Inc., Shelton; p. 35 courtesy of the U.S. Navy, Submarine Force Museum, Groton; p. 37 © Robert Levin; p. 39 © Peter Sispoidis; p. 41 © Robert Benson; p. 43 © Jeff Kaufman; p. 45 © John Artashian; p. 47 © Hitchcock Chair Co.; p. 49 courtesy of Devin Janosov; p. 51 © 2006 Jack McConnell; p. 53 © Robert Levin; p. 55 © Connecticut River Museum; p. 57 © www.johnmcolumbus.com; p. 59 © 2006 Jack McConnell; p. 61 courtesy of Yale Athletics Department; p. 65 © 2006 Jack McConnell; p. 67 © PEZ Candy, Inc.; p. 69 © Robert Levin; p. 71 courtesy of Travelers Property Casualty; p. 73 courtesy of Louis Belloisy; p. 75 © Robert Benson; p. 77 © 2006 Jack McConnell; p. 79 © Robert Levin; p. 81 © www.johnmcolumbus.com; p. 83 © Onne van der Wal, courtesy of Vanguard Sailboats; p. 85 courtesy of Connecticut Department of Transportation; p. 87 © www.johnmcolumbus.com; p. 89 © 2006 Jack McConnell; p. 91 courtesy of Mystic Seaport; p. 93 © Robert Benson; p. 95 © January 1996. Merritt Parkway; p. 97 © Robert Levin; p. 99 courtesy of General Cigar; p. 101 © 2006 Jack McConnell; p. 103 courtesy of Louis Belloisy.

Contents

Contents

Acknowledgments

One of the best things about initially having written these little stories for a magazine is that so many expert editorial eyes got to see them before publication. I'd like to thank my *Connecticut Magazine* colleagues (and friends) Dale Salm, Valerie Schroth, Pat Grandjean, Ray Bendici, Cathy Ross, and Audrey Brainerd for catching errors, suggesting better ways of saying things, and otherwise improving what they read.

Similarly, my thanks to the magazine's art director, Joan Barrow, and her assistants, Devin Janosov, Troy Monroe, and Becky Eller, for assigning or searching for and finding the right images to go with the words.

Mike Mims, *Connecticut Magazine*'s president and publisher, read every word of every Icon, made many valuable suggestions, always made sure that numbers, dimensions, and distances added up properly, and did what he had to do to get this book published. Thanks, Mike, I greatly appreciate all your efforts.

At The Globe Pequot Press, Mary Norris took an early interest in this book and stayed with it through thin and thick. Amy Paradysz and Sue Preneta enthusiastically led me through the publishing process and made sure everything turned out as it should.

Finally, my love and thanks to my wife, Marcia, and children, John, Matt, and Claire, who accompanied me on some of my travels around Connecticut and always (at least when I was watching) had the good manners to turn first to the last page of *Connecticut Magazine* when these Icon stories were regularly appearing there.

Introduction

If there is one thing I've learned about Connecticut after writing about it for the past thirty-five years, it is that it eludes easy definition. Like a mousy but keenly observant Jane Austen heroine, Connecticut sits between bigger-than-life New York ("the city that never sleeps") and self-absorbed Boston ("the hub of the universe"), learning much from both but taking up with neither. We are a small state, easily overlooked. Our natural gifts are better suited to the small screen than the large: murmuring streams, overgrown pastures, and fall foliage rather than snow-capped peaks, roaring surf, and raging wildfires. Similarly, our virtues—intelligence, refinement, and moderation, to name a few—almost by definition do not call attention to themselves.

Adding to this "definition" problem (if it is a problem) is the fact that, compared with other states, Connecticut has long been a nonstarter in the self-promotion game. For example:

- We must be alone among the fifty states in having a state song, "Yankee Doodle," that is not even about us.

- Our state university's mascot, the UConn Husky, has no particular local connection but rather comes as the result of an awkward play on words having to do with "Yukon."

- For years the state's only major-league sports team was called the Whalers, a name borrowed from an earlier day when the team was located in Boston. Our current major-league team, the women's pro basketball Suns, got its name from a South African casino mogul whose first name is Sol.

■ We are the "Constitution State," but few people know what that means; we are called "Nutmeggers," but few people know why.

■ Even though all the cities and most of the commerce and people are on our shore, the body of water that lies between Connecticut and New York is called Long Island Sound.

The list goes on and on, but in essence it all boils down to this: Here we sit between Rhode Island clam chowder and Manhattan clam chowder without a chowder to call our own.

So with all the foregoing in mind, I was happy to do my part on behalf of our state's good name by compiling this collection of Connecticut icons.

As I began working on these essays, most of which originally appeared on the back page of *Connecticut Magazine*, my thought was to build a picture of Connecticut piece by piece. As a native of the state, I knew that there were many familiar features of daily life here, things most of us see but take for granted, that could stand a closer look. We buzz by the tobacco sheds on our way to Bradley Airport, under an Art Deco bridge over the Merritt Parkway, or past the train station tower in Waterbury, glancing at them briefly and then moving on. We enjoy visiting Sleeping Giant

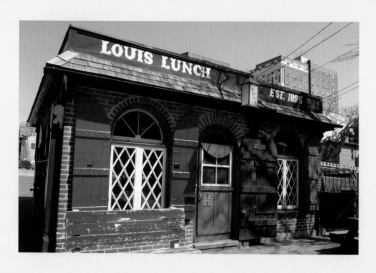

State Park, Candlewood Lake, or Hammonasset Beach, but we don't have a clue as to how they came to be. We bite into a Mounds bar, a hot lobster roll, or a white clam pizza unaware of the colorful Connecticut story behind each. I was delighted to find that there were lots of colorful stories.

The enjoyment in compiling these pieces came largely in the research and in placing each icon into its particular time in Connecticut history. In doing so, I didn't go at it as a trained historian but more like an enthusiast looking through old scrapbooks in the attic. If I were reading through newspapers on microfilm for information on the opening of Yale Bowl in 1914, for example, I'd invariably end up reading the whole paper, including the ads and comics. If I were doing an Internet search on the Hitchcock chair, I'd range so far afield that I sometimes had trouble getting back to the subject at hand.

Does this collection further the cause of defining our elusive little state? I don't know the answer to that, of course, but I'm hoping it will at least stir curiosity in readers and get them out exploring their own favorite things. As for Connecticut's identity, I am content with a definition I once found in a book published in the 1920s. I like it because it is as true today as it was on the day it was written, it cannot be challenged, and it is only thirteen words long. It reads, "Connecticut is slightly larger than Jamaica and a third as large as Switzerland."

The Thimble Islands

They say the Thimble Islands, that charming little archipelago off the Branford coast, got their name from a type of berry that grows there, but I think they get it from their ability to gather up and retain unlikely stories and legends.

Take, for example, the ubiquitous Captain Kidd, the seventeenth-century pirate who seems to have foolishly spent most of his time burying treasure in spots around Long Island Sound and very little time spending it. In the case of the Thimbles, Kidd is said to have used High Island as a headquarters and lookout and Money Island as a place to hide his loot in an underwater cavern—which of course remains undiscovered to this day.

According to other Thimbles legends, Horse Island is so named because a horse once swam to it from a shipwreck; Cut-in-Two Island was once home to a "beautiful midget" with whom Tom Thumb fell in love; and Pot Island was the playground of the nineteenth-century Fat Man's Club. Indeed, it seems that each of the islands (others include Bear, Little Pumpkin, Mother-in-Law, Hen, and Potato) has a story to tell, even if it's only how the island got its name.

■ You can book a Thimble Islands cruise at (203) 481-3345 or (203) 488-8905. ■

Depending upon your definition of what an island is, there are possibly more than 100 Thimbles, but only a couple of dozen are large enough to be inhabited. The Indian name for them translates to "beautiful sea rocks," and on a calm summer morning you can see why. With their pink granite heads poking above the high-water mark (barely, in some cases), they scatter like a handful of charms across the Sound from Indian Neck to Sachem's Head.

Together, the islands constitute one of Connecticut's most unusual and exclusive communities.

There are ninety-five dwellings among all the Thimbles, ranging from tiny cottages to substantial houses (twelve-acre Rogers Island has a mansion, guesthouse, boathouse, beach house, pool, and tennis court). Some of the islands are home to multiple dwellings, while others barely have room for one; in a few cases, a lone house sits possessively astride its rock like an insect on a bread crumb.

The residents, most of whom live here during summer months only, must get used to the quirks of island life. Everything, obviously, comes and goes by boat, so planning is key. Fresh water, on most islands, comes from wells, and electricity is supplied by generators. Some houses still employ kerosene lamps. Evening entertainment may well come from a deck of cards.

A few of the larger islands are not inhabited at all except by day-trippers and wildlife. Horse Island, at seventeen acres the largest of the Thimbles, is owned by Yale University and used for the study of marine biology. Likewise, five-acre Outer Island is part of the federal Stewart B. McKinney Wildlife Refuge and is also used as a site for study.

A Thimble Island doesn't come onto the market very often. Back in 1980, the twelve-acre Rogers Island could be had for $1.9 million, and in 1985 was on sale again for $3 million. There's no telling what such a treasure would fetch today. A couple of other islands were on the market recently. East Crib Island, with a 1,888-square-foot house perched on about a half acre and with mainland electricity, was listed at $4.5 million. Belden Island, with its 1912 Victorian farmhouse, could be yours for $4.25 million.

Such is the high price these days of beginning your own legend.

Dinosaur Mural

When I was a boy, especially if I was home from school and sick in bed, there was a book I turned to again and again for entertainment and companionship, the way kids now turn to their favorite PlayStation game. The book was *The World We Live In*, first published in 1955 by *Life* magazine. On its large pages were illustrations and photos that depicted nothing less than the formation of the universe and solar system, the evolution of our own planet, and the panoply of life on Earth.

Some of the images were particularly memorable. There was an illustration of the Earth as a boiling sea of lava. There was a full-page photo of a "giant grouper" that struck such fear into me, my brother, and my oldest sister (perhaps because the caption said it could swallow a child whole) that we attacked it repeatedly with whatever sharp objects we could find.

But most striking of all was the large-scale painting that showed the evolution of reptilian life on Earth, beginning more than 300 million years ago. In my febrile state, with a vaporizer bubbling in a corner of the room, I'd lie in bed and stare at these majestic, scrupulously detailed scenes: the flamboyant fan-finned beasts of the Permian Era; the looming brontosaurus opposite its miniature relative in the Jurassic; the ferocious *Tyrannosaurus rex*; and ominous steaming volcanoes in the Cretaceous. At length the book would fall onto my chest, and I'd dream horrifying, heroic dinosaur dreams.

■ For museum hours call (203) 432-5050. ■

It wasn't until years later that I realized the pictures in the book had been taken from an enormous mural at Yale's Peabody Museum, not 30 miles from my own front door. The artist was Rudolph F. Zallinger, a Russian emigré who'd been given the assignment when Peabody Director Albert Parr decided the museum walls looked rather colorless and bleak. Zallinger was a young man of twenty-two when he got the job in early 1942. He spent the first six months conferring with experts and then worked the next year or so making sketches and doing other preliminary work on his 110-foot-by-16-foot "canvas."

Zallinger began painting the mural in October 1943, and for the next three-and-a-half years he devoted most of his time to the project. As he worked, the museum's Great Hall remained open, and the public, including many of the students and faculty at Yale, was able to come in and view the ongoing spectacle of what would become know as "The Age of Reptiles."

When it was completed in June 1947, the mural was greeted with universal acclaim. Zallinger received the Pulitzer Prize for Painting, and he noted with pride that the day's most prominent authority on Renaissance murals, Daniel Varney Thompson, told another Yale professor, "That wall is the most important one since the fifteenth century."

The mural was reproduced in *Life* in 1952, beginning a long and fruitful relationship between the artist and the magazine. *Life* commissioned Zallinger to produce another work, "The Age of Mammals," in 1953. The new painting was published in October of that year but wasn't turned into a mural at the Peabody until the 1960s, when funds became available and Zallinger, who was then on the faculty at the Hartford Art School, could get started.

With the renewed interest in things reptilian over the past fifteen years, from *Jurassic Park* to Barney, it seems clear that "The Age of Reptiles" will never go out of style. Until stranger, fiercer creatures come along, dinosaurs will rule the fevered imaginations of young boys and girls, and the Peabody will remain one of the great places to go to imagine them walking the Earth.

Candlewood Lake

Imagine being there on that day in February 1928 when the flooding began—when they turned the switch and started pumping water from the Housatonic River up through the huge pipe (more than 13 feet in diameter) called a penstock, over a ridge, and into the Rocky River Valley to create Candlewood Lake.

The valley must have been eerily still that day, with nothing but ghosts left to witness the rising tide. Two years earlier, a man named Charles Campbell had gone door-to-door through the area, bargaining for and buying up property on behalf of the Connecticut Light & Power Company. Not that the inhabitants of doomed villages such as Jerusalem and Leach Hollow had much choice in the matter. Two decades earlier, the power company had been authorized by the General Assembly to develop the hydroelectric potential of the Housatonic River. Part of the master plan was the creation of an enormous lake that could hold water and release it when necessary for the generation of electricity. The official view, and eventual reality, was that this new power source would help ensure the continued growth and economic vitality of western Connecticut and its citizens. Campbell likely advised the residents of the valley that resistance was useless; the new lake was a done deal, and within a couple of years this farmhouse—*right where we're standing!*—will be under 40 feet of water. So the farmers, some of whose families had owned the land since before the American Revolution, sold at fair prices for the day—$2,356 for fifty-three acres, $3,000 for thirty-four acres, $100 for three acres—and got out.

With much of the valley thus abandoned, construction crews set up camp in the summer of 1926 and began building the 950-foot-long, 100-foot-high main dam and four smaller dikes that would

■ Candlewood Lake can be enjoyed at Squantz Pond State Park on Route 39 in New Fairfield. ■

eventually keep the waters of the new lake in place. An additional workforce of about 1,000 woodsmen, mostly from Maine and Canada, moved in to clear the 5,420-acre basin. Working without power tools, they demolished or moved more than one hundred buildings, cleared brush, and chopped down thousands of trees. For months, the air in the valley was thick with the smoke from huge bonfires of burning debris.

Even so, such was the rush to get the project under way that many reminders of life in what was once the Rocky River Valley were left behind. As the water poured in at the rate of about a million gallons every four minutes, it crept across and covered dirt roads and bridges, farming implements, bicycles and an old jalopy, two cemeteries (the bodies had been removed), a schoolhouse, and the foundations of numerous summer cottages and farmhouses.

The flooding of the basin continued for seven months until it topped out at 440 feet above sea level. The new lake was the largest in Connecticut. It was 11 miles long and 2 miles across at its widest point and reached a depth of 85 feet.

Most interesting of all, it provided the towns of New Fairfield, Sherman, New Milford, Brookfield, and Danbury with 60 new miles of shoreline. For a brief period, the lake and the surrounding land remained in a stunning, near-pristine state, but soon enough reality set in, and the area became a summer playground and eventually a coveted spot for year-round living.

These days, the surface of the lake buzzes loudly with every sort of motorized craft, but deep below the surface in the province of the fishes and an occasional diver, the old farming valley quietly abides.

Mounds Bar

When the American doughboys returned from Europe after fighting in World War I, it was with a heightened appreciation for a couple of things they had experienced overseas. One was the shocking openness of French women, as immortalized in "Mademoiselle from Armentieres" ("You might forget the gas and shell/But you'll never forget the Mademoiselle"), and the other was the taste of American chocolate bars.

Chocolate had for some time been a staple treat for soldiers in combat, but during WWI the men were for the first time provided with individual bars they could easily fit into their backpacks. The revolutionary rectangle of chocolate was made by the Hershey Company in Pennsylvania, which had been producing its Hershey bar since 1900. If the return-ing veterans could aspire to French women only as increasingly distant memories, they could certainly satisfy their new craving for choco-late bars—and quickly spread it among their families and friends. Needless to say, American ingenuity was more than prepared to rise to the challenge.

> ■ Tours of the Naugatuck Peter Paul factory in which Mounds are made can be arranged by calling (203) 720-4200. ■

It was thus that the 1920s became the great Golden Age of the American candy bar. The decade began with the introduction of the Baby Ruth (named after former President Cleveland's daugh-ter, not the Yankee slugger), followed by Oh Henry! in 1921, Charleston Chew and Reese's Peanut Butter Cup in 1922, Butterfinger and Milky Way in 1923, Bit-O-Honey in 1924, Mr. Goodbar in 1925, Milk Duds in 1926, Mike & Ike in 1927, Heath Bar in 1928, and Snickers in 1929. With alcohol taken away by Prohibition, it seemed Americans had turned en masse to candy as a means of sinful escape.

Getting into the game early was a group of Armenian emigrés living in Connecticut. Peter Paul Halajian had been making chocolates in his home and selling them from small shops he owned in the Naugatuck Valley. Before long, Halajian was persuaded by his brother-in-law to plunge fully into the wholesale candy business. With backing from fellow countrymen, he established the Peter Paul Manufacturing Company in New Haven in 1919.

The first product, the Konabar, was a blend of coconut, fruits, nuts, and chocolate. The Mounds bar, consisting of sweetened coconut and bittersweet chocolate, was introduced in 1920. Mounds was an immediate hit. Within two years, the fledgling company was forced to move to a larger facility in Naugatuck just to keep up with the demand. In the years that followed, some new products (Almond Cluster, Caravelle, No Jelly) came and went, while one notable entry (Almond Joy, introduced in 1946) became a star in its own right. Corporate acquisitions have made their marks over time. Peter Paul bought the maker of Walnettos candy way back in 1929 and of York Peppermint Patties in 1972. The company was in turn merged with Cadbury in 1978 and eventually purchased by Hershey Foods in 1988.

Today, Mounds bars are made nowhere else but in Naugatuck. The plant, occupying the same site on New Haven Road as it did in 1922, employs about 270 people and churns out four sizes of Mounds, along with Almond Joy and Classic Caramels.

The doughboys may all have gone on to that great big French dance hall in the sky, but one of the things they left behind—the Mounds bar—is a deliciously sweet legacy.

Berlin Turnpike

As Connecticut's economy completed the transition from farming to manufacturing, its cities grew dirtier, noisier, and more crowded, and the people who lived in them began looking for ways to get out.

One means of escape arrived at the beginning of the twentieth century with the expansion of urban light-rail lines, taking trolleys and their riders out of the cities and into the countryside. By 1915, for example, a boy in Waterbury could get on a trolley in his home city and, several hours (and transfers) later, disembark for a day of swimming at an East Haven beach. Indeed, to lure city dwellers into frequenting their trolleys, the companies often built an amusement park at the end of the line, which is how Quassy Amusement Park in Middlebury got its start in 1908.

■ You can read about the Berlin Turnpike and see lots of great vintage photos in *Route 15: The Road to Hartford* by Larry Larned. ■

But even as the trolleys were enjoying their heyday, people all across Connecticut were discovering the infinitely more satisfying and lasting pleasures of the automobile. As affordable, reliable cars flooded the marketplace, the state hustled to provide a system of paved roads to accommodate them.

As the years went by and the network of good roads grew more complex, certain stretches of highway began to stand out for the services and pleasures they offered to the motoring public. Sections of the Post Road between Stamford and New Haven were notable in this respect, as were parts of U.S. Route 6, but perhaps the best-known and most beloved by many for its raffish charm was, and is, the Berlin Turnpike.

By Connecticut standards, the Berlin Turnpike is a remarkably straight road. It runs some 11 miles between Meriden and Wethersfield, a vestige of the Hartford and New Haven Turnpike that opened in 1799 and was considered unusual for not following the winding old roads of earlier days.

Although well traveled as a part of U.S. Route 5, the Berlin Turnpike really came into its own in the early 1940s, when it became the heavily commercialized link between two sections of the limited-access Wilbur Cross Parkway, also to be known as Route 15. Here, motorists could find road-houses, beaneries, motor hotels (later shortened to "motels"), bowling alleys, drive-in movies, wild-animal farms, and gas stations—lots and lots of gas stations. The Berlin Turnpike gas-price wars became so famous that the road was also known as Gasoline Alley.

Today, many of the eccentric old road-side attractions have disappeared, replaced in large part by box retailers and shopping centers. But you can still play a round of miniature golf along the turnpike or a game of laser tag. You can still head out for a big meal or visit bars fea-turing "exotic" dancers, and there are motels galore, including the legendary Grantmoor, with its provocatively themed guest rooms. You can even stop in at the Olympia Diner for a bite to eat. Opened in 1952, the Olympia holds its neon banner high, beckoning the hungry and the restless in off the road for a cup of coffee and a piece of pie.

In some ways, the Berlin Turnpike still serves as a means of retreat from the world at large. On weekends, it is now home to a significant cruise scene, as hundreds of vintage cars and trucks make their way back and forth out on the blacktop, a faint echo of our unspoken deal with the roads we build—that they will take us someplace we haven't been, show us things we haven't seen, and keep alive our dreams of escape.

Blue-Blazed Trails

As a lifelong resident of Connecticut and someone who professes to enjoy the outdoors, I am ashamed to admit that I'd never set foot on one of the state's blue-blazed trails until a recent Sunday, when my wife and I parked our car in Peterson Memorial Park in Wolcott, walked past a skateboard park, and started out along an old woods road that constitutes the southern end of the 38-mile Mattatuck Trail.

Within minutes the road narrowed to a well-worn path, and the sounds of the outside world began to fade behind us, replaced by the babbling of the Mad River, whose streamlike headwaters meandered gently beside us. A few minutes later, as we neared the confluence of the Mad and another, even smaller rill, we found ourselves entering an open area that I wouldn't have associated with Wolcott at all: towering hemlocks, filtered sunlight, tumbling and splashing water, and an understory of moss-covered boulders, ferns, and mountain laurel. It was like a big, green outdoor room, an immediate Favorite Place that was ten minutes from our front door.

■ There are more than 700 miles of blue-blazed trails in the state; see www.ctwoodlands.org/bluetrails.html. ■

As we stood there, taking it all in, I felt the sudden rush of an epiphany: Hiking will now officially take the place of golf. The shaky putter will be replaced by the solid walking stick. Frustration and anger will give way to peace and serenity. Life will get measurably better. With the wild-eyed look of an instant convert, I turned to my wife and told her that I wanted to walk all the blue-blazed trails of Connecticut—all 700 miles of them. For if the Mattatuck Trail could offer up such a treasure in its first half-mile, I said, there's no telling what other surprises might await along the Nipmuck, the Mattabesett, the Pachaug, and the Tunxis.

Afterall, what better way could there be to celebrate Connecticut's blue-blazed trail system than by getting out and walking it? What better way to acknowledge the efforts of all the volunteers, who since 1929 have blazed and maintained these trails, than by hiking, rather than driving, through the glorious October foliage this year? And what better first step to take than to order the *Connecticut Walk Book*, the hiker's bible?

Besides an exhaustive set of notes on and maps of every trail in the state, the *Walk Book* helpfully explains that the state's trail system began as an offshoot of the Connecticut Forest and Park Association (CFPA), which had been founded in 1895 to oversee the preservation, enhancement, and maintenance of the state's natural resources. The first trail was the Quinnipiac in 1931; as it does today, it ran north from Mount Carmel in Hamden, across Sleeping Giant State Park and Mad Man's Hill, and up into Cheshire. By 1934, the CFPA volunteers had developed some 400 miles of trails. Since then, new trails have been added and some old ones altered or discontinued, usually because of the encroachments of civilization (most of the trail mileage runs through private, rather than public, lands). But through it all, the trails have stayed true to their original purpose: to provide a nearby, temporary escape from the vicissitudes of life.

"The trails were established in proximity to settled areas for a reason," reads a recent piece in *Connecticut Woodlands,* a CFPA publication. "That was that a life without the regular chance to walk through a natural setting is a diminished one. The point of Connecticut's trails was to connect us to nature where we live."

And so they do, brilliantly. See you in the woods.

Chester-Hadlyme Ferry

In the culture of New England, reliability is held as a virtue nearly on a level with godliness and cleanliness. When the newspaper lands on the doorstep every morning, when the lawnmower starts right up after a long winter's storage, when the rooster crows or the robin returns, or when Richard Blumenthal announces he will not be running for governor—these are signal moments that can bring genuine pleasure to the classically inclined New Englander.

So it is with the Chester-Hadlyme Ferry, which has faithfully plied the waters of the Connecticut River since 1769. At first glance it would seem a small thing, this constant running back and forth across a stretch of river. Yet in how many other places can you still observe and even take part in a ritual that began more than 230 years ago?

■ The river ferry is accessible on both the Chester and Hadlyme sides of the Connecticut River on Route 148; call (860) 443-3856. ■

Of course, ferry service along the Connecticut goes back a lot further than that. For hundreds of years, the Native Americans left their canoes at strategic hiding places along the riverbanks. The first ferry piloted by white settlers was launched from Windsor in 1641, followed by other important operations between Saybrook and Old Lyme, Middletown and Portland, and Haddam and East Haddam. The ferry linking Rocky Hill and Glastonbury was established in 1655 and continues today as the oldest continuously operating ferry crossing in the United States and as the only other river ferry still running in Connecticut.

The Chester-Hadlyme service was originally called Warner's Ferry, named for Jonathan Warner, who owned the land on both sides of the river and established a tavern on the Hadlyme side.

The boat itself was basically a barge that ferrymen propelled with long poles and brute strength; it proved its worth during the Revolutionary War by carrying supplies and troops in aid of the rebel cause.

By the late 1800s, steam power had been introduced, and in 1882 the ferry was taken over by the Town of Chester. In 1915, the state Highway Department assumed control of the ferry, including whatever annual deficit it runs, which in recent years has been around $100,000.

On a recent spring Sunday afternoon, we drove to Chester to take a ride across the river. When we got there, four cars were waiting at the landing, and we could see *Selden III* just pulling out of the Hadlyme side. The 65-foot-long boat was built in 1949 and can accommodate up to nine cars and forty-nine passengers. We were the only foot passengers. We paid $1.50 each for the round-trip and walked on board.

Claire Monagan, 13, surreptitiously jotted down notes during the trip. Here were her findings, later revealed under the heading "Ferry Stuff":

"Used to be useful in old days . . . bridge very far either side—convenient for some cars . . . boat goes slow . . . Chester, Hadlyme are the towns on either side (Chester like a dollhouse town) . . . river 11 feet at greatest depth . . . Gillette Castle on hill up high . . . no indoor area for passengers . . . Lifejackets (6 children, 71 adult) . . . one way in 3 minutes 45 seconds."

If she had the time, she might also have mentioned the fresh breeze, the lovely turns in the river, the surrounding green hills, and the feeling of taking a place in a line that stretches back to Connecticut's earliest days. It's one of the state's great cheap thrills.

The Colt .45

Connecticut has never been shy about creating, producing, and selling weapons of destruction—mass or otherwise. Perhaps we suffer from a small state's Napoleonic complex, but according to *Connecticut Firsts* by Wilson Faude and Joan Friedland, we built the first American warship and the first ballistic-missile submarine, and we invented floating mines, underwater torpedos, the repeating rifle, Gatling gun, automatic pistol, gun silencer, and bazooka rocket gun.

Our most famous contribution to the arsenal, however, got its start in 1836, when Samuel Colt was issued a U.S. patent for a firearm equipped with a revolving cylinder. In expert hands, the revolutionary revolver allowed its user to wound several people in quick succession or deliver a series of deadly slugs to a single person—to "fill him with lead," as the saying went. With the new gun in hand, it wasn't long before U.S. Dragoon forces and Texas Rangers were reporting back to

■ The Colt collection of firearms is on display at the Museum of Connecticut History in Hartford; call (860) 757-6535. ■

their superiors in Washington that their Colt sidearms were highly effective in subjugating the Western Indian tribes. When it came to fighting Mexicans a year or so later, however, the War Department wanted something a little more powerful, and Colt was happy to oblige. He and Captain Samuel H. Walker collaborated on the Walker revolver, the first Colt gun to be manufactured in Connecticut.

Such inventions and innovations eventually made Colt a business hero and a very rich man. He purchased hundreds of acres in the South Meadows of Hartford for the construction of his massive armory, including its iconic blue onion dome, and housing for Colt workers in a complex that was to be known as Coltsville. In 1855, he began building Armsmear, an ornate Gilded Age mansion that he lived in with his wife, Elizabeth, and ne'er-do-well son, Caldwell.

But Samuel Colt was not one to rest on his laurels. Right up to his death in 1862, at the age of forty-eight, he sought to supply the world with larger, faster, and more lethal guns—and he really didn't seem to care how, or to whom, he sold them. According to William Hosley's *Colt: The Making of an American Legend,* his "most controversial 'marketing' technique involved combinations of bribery, black-mail, bullying and baiting." In anticipation of the carnage of the Civil War, Colt sold as many weapons as he could to both the North and South sides. He sold to the British and Russians during the Crimean War and to the Mexicans after they were defeated by the United States but still posed a border threat.

The company's most illustrious achievement, the Colt Peacemaker, didn't come along until the 1870s. It was originally issued as a .44-calibre gun, but, again, the Army wanted something more powerful, and the Colt .45 was born. The gun became a symbol of the Wild West and found its way into the hands of such notables as Wyatt Earp, General George Custer, Doc Holiday, and Bat Masterson. The Colt .45 semi-automatic pistol became the Army's sidearm of choice during both World War I and World War II, when the company delivered some 2.5 million units to the government.

These days, of course, the Colt .45 pistol has long since been supplanted as a top weapon in combat. It does live on as a collectible or, with fancy grips and engravings, as a showpiece. Collectors like them, I suppose, in part because they summon up a simpler, more pleasant day, a time when people were content to kill each other one at a time.

UConn Dairy Bar

If, in some completely unforeseen Armageddon, it all comes down to a battle between the UConn Huskies and the UConn Holsteins, you can put me squarely on the side of the ruminants. The Huskies, as we all know, play their games at facilities on campus or the big new football stadium in East Hartford. The Holsteins, on the other hand, are restricted to the fields on Horsebarn Hill in Storrs, where they graze placidly, swat flies with their tails, and produce the milk for what many believe to be the best ice cream in Connecticut.

In these days of big-time athletics and billion-dollar campus building projects, it is instructive to recall that the University of Connecticut began its life in 1881 as an agricultural college. Because the state's rocky soil and hilly terrain made it a far better place for dairy farming than, say, growing wheat, many of the classes taught in Storrs in those days had to do with dairy husbandry. Courses seemed to resemble chores—milk production and separation, ice cream making, butter and cheese making—not what we now think of today as college courses.

■ The UConn Dairy Bar is open year-round; call (860) 486-2634 for hours and flavors. ■

In order for students to properly learn these and other techniques, a dairy herd was established, barns and related buildings went up, other types of livestock were brought in, and soon a busy working farm became the center of campus life.

One of the more popular offshoots of the farm's dairy operation was a campus creamery. At its mid-twentieth-century peak, the creamery employed more than twenty-five full-time workers and grossed more than a million dollars a year. In a delightful example of sensible governance, it supplied the UConn dorms and other state agencies with daily deliveries of fresh milk, sour cream, cream cheese, and ice cream. The creamery ended most of its operations in 1991 after nearly a century of service.

But the Dairy Bar remains. Even as UConn has exploded into a major research university and as its agricultural component recedes into a kind of pleasant background noise, the thriving Dairy Bar remains open to the public, serving as a link to the school's bucolic origins.

Opened fifty years ago as the Dairy Product Salesroom, the Dairy Bar these days resembles an actual commercial ice cream shop, but with one major difference: At the rear of the room is a large viewing window through which, at certain times of day, visitors can watch the ice cream–making process.

Visitors are welcome to tour UConn's animal barns as well. The farm on Horsebarn Hill remains vital to the university's Animal Science Department (at present sixty students strong) and is home to more than 200 Holstein and Jersey cows, 40 swine, 40 brood ewes, 55 mature beef cattle, 85 horses and 1,000 poultry. The tours of the barns are self-guided and free, and there are even picnic tables along the way.

Of course, the only acceptable way to end a tour of the farm is with a cup of ice cream, or a cone, or sundae, or shake, from the Dairy Bar. The portions are generous, the prices are reasonable, the service friendly, and the ice cream creamy and delicious. Perhaps best of all, you can take your treat outside and stroll back over to the enormous sloping pasture that defines Horsebarn Hill. There you may find a dreamy late summer scene, with the crickets chirping lazily in the hay and the herd lowing in the golden distance. And like any good UConn fan, you may find yourself wanting to shout:

Go Holsteins!

The Sleeping Giant

Connecticut's natural wonders ordinarily do not inspire postcards or specials on the Discovery Channel. They tend to be modest and charming in a Southern New England sort of way rather than grand and awesome. We have Kent Falls, not Niagara Falls; rolling green hills rather than snow-capped peaks; Bigelow Hollow, not the Grand Canyon. But there is at least one natural feature that in my experience never fails to move a young person seeing it for the first time, usually from the back seat of a car driving north from New Haven along Interstate 91: The Sleeping Giant.

Geologically speaking, the Giant is, in the words of Michael Bell's indispensable book *The Face of Connecticut*, "a traprock colossus sacked out forever in the Central Valley brownstone." The five ridges in Hamden that make up the Giant are composed of durable, red-hued traprock—as are several other notable hills and ridges in central Connecticut—their contours shaped but not worn away by the comings and goings of various glaciers.

No one knows, of course, when the first person might have looked at the formation of the ridges and said, "Hey, that looks just like a . . . *sleeping giant!*" But there is a Native American legend that, according to *Born Among the Hills: The Sleeping Giant Story* by Nancy Davis Sachse, speaks of a rather large, irritable spirit named Hobbomock who stamped his foot and caused the abrupt turn of the Connecticut River to the east at Middletown.

■ Sleeping Giant State Park is located just off Route 10 in Hamden; call (860) 424-3200. ■

To keep Hobbomock in line and prevent such monumental hissy fits in the future, a good spirit named Kietan cast a spell and put him to sleep forever.

By the late nineteenth century, the Hamden ridges, with their fresh air and pleasant views, became a fashionable place for New Haven residents to construct their summer cottages. In 1912, however, one of the landowners leased his property to the Mt. Carmel Traprock Company, which immediately began quarrying on the area generally thought of as the Giant's head. This caused not only a severe disfigurement that remains visible to this day but also an uproar that eventually led to the formation of the Sleeping Giant Park Association (SGPA) in 1924 and finally to the end to all quarrying in 1933.

Today, the SGPA remains a presence at what is now known as Sleeping Giant State Park, one of the real gems in Connecticut's park system. The association maintains some 30 miles of excellent hiking trails and is also responsible for producing a very useful guidebook to the park's nature trail. Other features at Sleeping Giant include a bridle path, a cross-country ski trail, and a sturdy Norman-style stone tower constructed on the Giant's left hip in 1936–1939 by the federal Works Progress Administration.

As long as Hobbomock slumbers peacefully, the tower and the pleasures of the park surrounding it should last for generations to come.

The Glass House

Connecticut has always been fertile ground for signature houses.

◼ Samuel Clemens spent many happy years, and a few sad ones, in his extraordinary Victorian (1874), now a museum on Farmington Avenue in Hartford.

◼ William Gillette took great pleasure in his eccentric castle (1919), now a state park overlooking the Connecticut River in East Haddam.

◼ Samuel Colt, P. T. Barnum, and scores of ambitious but lesser-known industrialists, corporate tycoons, entertainers, swindlers, and spendthrift heirs have spent untold millions building enormous multi-roomed, multi-chimneyed monuments to themselves—each larger than the last, and each conceived with the idea of leaving behind something that would draw attention for many decades to come.

Yet the boldest statement of them all and the one that may best stand up to the test of time is also the simplest: the glass house that the iconoclastic architect Philip Johnson built for himself in New Canaan.

Johnson, who died in 2005 at the age of ninety-eight, came out to Fairfield County from New York City at the end of World War II, a few years after he'd received a degree in architecture from Harvard at the advanced age of thirty-eight.

◼ The Glass House is not yet open to the public, but you can find out more about it at www.greatbuildings.com/buildings/Johnson_House.html. ◼

He liked the lay of the land in New Canaan and the price he could get it for, so he bought five acres and began work on what would be called "one of the masterworks of modern American architecture."

It is said that Johnson borrowed the basic concept for his new house from Mies van der Rohe, who was designing the glass-and-steel Farnsworth House in Illinois at around the same time. But Johnson finished his first, in 1949, and it has stood ever since as the very essence of "modern," even as it moves toward its sixtieth birthday. The few divisions within the glass and steel box come from low walnut cabinets and a brick cylinder that contains the bathroom. The brick floor and the cylinder were waxed to give them a purplish color, the steel was painted dark gray, and the steps and railings were made from white granite.

"The serene Glass House, a 56-foot-by-32-foot rectangle, is generally considered one of the twentieth century's greatest residential structures," wrote architectural critic Paul Goldberger on the occasion of Johnson's death. "Like all of Johnson's early work, it was inspired by Mies, but its pure symmetry, dark colors and closeness to the earth marked it as a personal statement: calm and ordered rather than sleek and brittle."

Almost in defiance of expectations, Johnson found his Glass House to be a place in which he could live comfortably. He became a familiar figure around town, had an office there for a while, and even served on the board of the New Canaan Historical Society.

And now, in death, Johnson will join Clemens and Gillette in having his house turned over to the public as a place they can learn from and enjoy. Perhaps in thanks for the life New Canaan allowed him, Johnson donated the entire estate to the National Trust for Historic Preservation, stipulating that the structures and grounds be opened as a museum upon his death. National Trust officials say it will be at least a couple of years before that happens, but the planning is under way.

Lastly, an aside to all would-be monument builders: Sometimes simple wins the day.

The Ninth Hole at Yale

Whenever knowledgeable golfers are asked to name the best, most difficult, or most memorable golf holes in Connecticut, the ninth at the Yale Golf Club always heads the list. Whether it's actually the best or the most difficult hole is open to endless debate, but it certainly is memorable. It's not only a pleasure to look at and a real challenge to play, but it's a genuine throwback to the very earliest days of the game.

In 1924, a 700-acre piece of property several miles west of the main campus was given to Yale by Mrs. Ray Tompkins in memory of her husband, the 1883 football team captain. The purpose of the gift was to create a new "Yale playground," including land to be used for "tramping, tobogganing and skiing" as well as for natural-history field studies. But according to the wishes of Tompkins himself, the bulk of the property was to be used for a new golf course.

The university went out and hired renowned course architect Charles Blair Macdonald, who fifteen years earlier had designed and built the country's first clearly strategic layout, the National Golf Links of America, at Southhampton on Long Island. By the mid-1920s, Macdonald had hooked up with a brilliant collaborator, Seth Raynor, and had also brought in as an assistant Charles Banks, a Yalie from the Class of '06, who had been off teaching at the Hotchkiss School for seventeen years.

■ Arrangements to play the Yale Golf Course can be made by calling (203) 432-0895. ■

Given this huge chunk of land and the lordly sum of $400,000 to spend on it, Macdonald and Raynor (evidence now suggests it was more the latter) drew up a classic layout over very difficult terrain. It was a course built on a massive scale, with broad fairways, gaping bunkers, and large, heavily contoured greens. Several holes have become classics, most notably the flamboyantly challenging fourth and tenth holes. It is the ninth, though, that golfers never seem to forget.

In the arcane terminology of golf architecture, the hole is known as a "Biarritz," because it resembles a famous par 3 designed in 1888 by Scotsman Willie Dunn for a course at the old French sea-side resort. A Biarritz features a long carry over a serious hazard to a huge green fronted by a deep swale. Macdonald and Raynor often built one into the courses they designed.

The hole at Yale is 215 yards long, with the tee situated 60 feet above Greist Pond. A shot must carry about 180 yards over the water before landing, if all goes well, on a putting surface that is 60 yards long from front to back and cut in half by a swale about 4 feet deep. In a true Biarritz setup, the hole is always located in the rear portion of the green, forcing all players to negotiate the swale. But Yale has not always been attuned to its course's great history, and the flag today is as likely to be located on the front of the green as it is in the rear.

Still, to play the ninth—and the rest of the Yale course—is to stir the echoes of an earlier day, and to par it is heaven.

Hot Lobster Roll

Connecticut's greatest contribution to the world of regional cuisine was born in 1934 or so in a little seafood shack called Perry's on the Post Road in Milford.

It was there that a liquor salesman, whose name is long forgotten, used to come in and ask proprietor Harry Perry to make him something special—a sandwich consisting of nothing more than hot lobster meat, melted butter, and bread.

Perry, who until 1929 had run a fish market down by the water, knew well the great appeal of lobster. As his little place out on the highway (then the main truck and auto route through southern Connecticut) began to grow into something more permanent, he decided to make the salesman's sandwich a regular part of his menu.

Correctly sensing that the hot, buttery meat needed to be held by something stronger than slices of bread, he ordered rolls from the French Bakery in Stratford. "They were shaped like hot dog rolls, but were chewier and more substantial, not like the cottony ones you get today," recalls Perry's granddaughter, Wendy Weir, who years later worked at Perry's as a teenager.

Perry picked the meat from the lobsters himself and prepared the rolls, four at a time, on a small grill. They were nothing like the lobster rolls then found elsewhere in New England, especially in Maine, which were—and still are—served cold and made with a salad of lobster meat, mayonnaise, and chopped celery. Perry's Connecticut version—with its dripping butter, tumbling chunks of

■ Lenny and Joe's Fish Tale can be found on the Post Road in Madison, (203) 245-7289, and Westbrook, (860) 669-0767. Abbott's is on Pearl Street in Noank, (860) 536-7719. ■

warm lobster, and sinfully rich, disintegrating bread—was a purer, more sensual treat; it seemed best devoured with big bites and a real sense of urgency.

The new sandwich was an instant success. In time, a big, bright neon sign went up at Perry's that said HOME OF THE FAMOUS LOBSTER ROLL. Harry Perry tried and failed to get a patent on his creation, and versions of it soon began to appear at other places along the shore. Still, through the 1940s and 1950s, even after the Merritt Parkway and Connecticut Turnpike pulled the long-haul traffic off the Post Road, everyone in Milford and well beyond knew about Perry's.

Perry turned over the restaurant to his son in 1962, and the place shut down altogether in 1976. Today another restaurant occupies the space in Milford, but the hot lobster roll lives on in dozens of seafood restaurants all across Connecticut, and each seems to have its own band of vocal supporters.

Among the most popular is the one served at Lenny and Joe's Fish Tale on Route 1 in Westbrook and Madison, where—as had become customary—a generous amount of meat is stuffed into a toasted New England-style, split-top hot dog roll. A variation with an equally devoted following is served at Abbott's Lobster-in-the-Rough in Noank with a round roll.

According to Wendy Weir, however, neither of these pretenders—nor any of the others up and down the coast—is quite up to the original lobster roll served by her grandfather in Milford. She claims there was a secret in the procedure at Perry's that she has never seen employed by another purveyor. "I still hold out hope," she says, only half-joking, "that some place will pay me to find out what it is."

Church on the Green

If the village green is Connecticut's most persistent reminder of its proper New England upbringing, the nearby white-steepled church comes in a close second. For well over 200 years, the soaring spires have peeked over treetops and stood like sentinels along curves in the road from one end of the state to the other, creating a powerful, highly visible community for all to ponder.

When the English first came to settle in this region, the Congregational church was the center of social and political as well as religious life. Their first meetinghouses were modest, houselike affairs, often square in shape and topped by a belfry. As the towns and congregations grew upward, however, so did their aspirations and their churches.

Among the oldest Connecticut survivors that exemplify this Gothic yearning for height are the churches built in Wethersfield, Farmington, and Brooklyn. The Brooklyn church (pictured) was built by the local Congregational Society but was taken over by the Unitarians in 1819 following a church schism. The double tiers of pedimented windows and tall tower with five stories of windows and open belfry stand as an excellent example of eighteenth-century New England church architecture.

The real golden age of church architecture came to Connecticut between 1810 and 1830. Dozens of new buildings were erected on town greens all across the state. Among the early examples were Center Church in New Haven (1812) designed by Ithiel Town, and, even more influentially, its next-door neighbor, United Church (1813) designed by David Hoadley. In the years that followed, Hoadley's designs graced the landscape in Avon (1818) and Milford (1823), where his church was later to be called "the ultimate masterpiece among our churches." His influence is plainly seen as well in Killingworth (1820), Cheshire (1826), and Southington (1828). Even the much-admired church on the green in Litchfield (1829) is a near copy of places that came before it, with its four fluted columns, three equal doors, and steeple with two octagonal stages—one open, one closed—and lofty spire.

Other churches around the state became known for a variety of reasons. The spire in Madison led mariners straight to the local harbor, and the church in Kensington was the first in Connecticut to install an organ, much to the consternation of many parishioners. When fixed atop an earlier spire, the weathervane atop the church in Newtown was riddled by musket balls fired by Rochambeau's bored French troops as they awaited orders during the Revolutionary War. There's an Eli Terry clock in the tower in—where else?—Terryville, and the church in Old Lyme was painted by many of the American Impressionists who lived and worked nearby, most famously Childe Hassam.

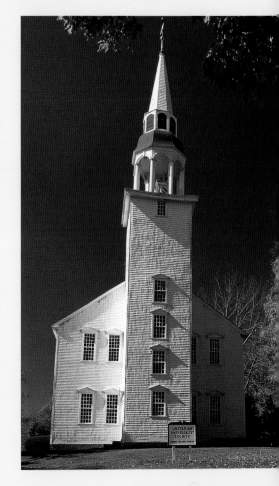

After 1830, church building continued, but the slender grace of earlier works was overtaken by a heavier, though by no means unattractive, Greek Revival style and any combination of styles thereafter. It's impressive that most of the churches built so long ago remain in use today, still drawing people in for introspection and inspiration, for a sense of sanctuary and belonging, and, of course, for coffee and gossip. Take a trip in early winter along the back roads of Connecticut, and you will see these churches everywhere—in Warren and Woodstock, Easton and Bethany, Wilton and Woodbury—their steeples lit up against the late-afternoon darkness, their windows and doors festooned with seasonal greenery. Be sure to notice them. Collectively, they could constitute Connecticut's greatest treasure.

Wiffle Ball

No one over the age of ten would ever think of our backyard as a baseball field. To begin with, there are five or six big oak trees with overhanging branches that create a low, trajectory-altering canopy. Substantial rocks protrude everywhere, getting in the way of sharply hit grounders and making backing up for a fly ball a dangerous sport. Sprawling rhododendrons intrude down the first-base line, ready to swallow a ball or poke out an eye. The yard tilts noticeably from home plate down toward the street beyond center field. The grass is almost never cut to the proper length for play. All in all, it's a terrible place to play, an unimaginable place to play.

Yet, on nice mornings in spring and fall before the school bus came or on long summer evenings as I tended to the nearby grill, the yard became a battlefield for countless games among our three children—a humble stage for muffed pop-ups and brilliant one-handed grabs, obnoxious home-run trots and belly-first slides, of triumph and shame, laughter, and tears and many, many disputes, until eventually a sort of grace settled over the place.

The one thing that turned our cramped little space into a field of dreams was the Wiffle ball, that marvelous white sphere of equal parts plastic, air, and magic dust. The ball was first produced in Shelton in 1953 by David N. Mullany, who invented it in just about the way you would have guessed: He spotted his son David and a friend playing pitcher/batter using a perforated plastic golf ball that for a variety of reasons was not getting the job done. He decided the boys needed a better ball, so he found some pieces of plastic at a nearby perfume factory and tinkered with them until he came up with a prototype of his own that was light enough to curve and dip, even when gently tossed, yet strong enough to endure a steady pounding. The company, still located in the same spot in Shelton and still in the Mullany family, today produces a few million balls a year, along with yellow plastic bats, a couple of other plastic toys, and, ironically, perforated golf balls.

In the fifty years since the ball was invented, Wiffle ball has become an ingrained part of our recreational lives. Most little kids learn to hit a Wiffle ball (usually with a huge plastic bat) long before they see a real baseball. Older kids and young adults enjoy it, too. Today there are leagues and tournaments all over America. Countless Web sites track the action, and something called the United States Perforated Plastic Baseball Association attempts to oversee it all. You can buy aluminum Wiffle ball bats with names like King Stick and Wiffle Pro, and the carbon-graphite Moonshot goes for around $120. Finally there are the fields—manicured, uniform (no rocks, no overhanging oak trees), with real outfield fences and lights for night play. I've even read of a Wiffle ball complex of twenty-two fields in Mishawaka, Indiana.

On the whole, however, I think I'll take our backyard. There hasn't been a game played there in years, but it's hard for me to think of it as anything but "the field." When I'm out mowing the lawn, I always take note of the bare spots that once designated the pitcher's mound and batter's box. I hope the grass never grows back.

The *Nautilus*

Connecticut's long and ardent romance with the Industrial Revolution reached its apotheosis in the summer of 1952, when Harry Truman traveled from the White House to Groton to lay the keel of the *Nautilus*.

Since the beginning of the nineteenth century, the vast output of the state's factories—the bright rivers of buttons and clocks, of pistols and locks, and more—had made fortunes for some and provided a decent life for many thousands. Now it was as if all those decades of ingenuity and effort had merely been in preparation for this one magnificent piece of work. Here on the Electric Boat Company's enormous staging floor would come together all the elements of the nuclear dream: the theories of Einstein and applications of Fermi; the power-plant designs and prototypes of research scientists from the Argonne National Laboratory in Illinois and Westinghouse Corp. engineers in Idaho; the strategic needs of the U.S. Navy as championed by Captain Hyman Rickover; and the skilled hands and strong backs of the workers at the boatyard.

■ The *Nautilus* is on view at the Submarine Force Library and Museum in Groton, (860) 694-3174. ■

Up until then, submarines had been nothing much more than diesel-powered boats that could also go underwater. They were awkward and slow, and they could stay below the surface only as long as their batteries allowed. By comparison, the *Nautilus* was to be fueled by the atom. As if by some half-crazy twentieth-century miracle, she would be able to run forever underwater or at least until the sailors' food and air supplies ran out. She'd run at unprecedented speeds, too. At a time when Stalin and Mao were in their heydays, this new ship would be something for the Soviets and Red Chinese to ponder. Here was America at the top of its game. And if all went well, who knew what other nuclear dreams might come true?

So Truman, who knew well the transforming power of the atom, initialed the keelpiece with chalk and pronounced it well laid. A year-and-a-half later, in January 1954, Mamie Eisenhower came to Connecticut to break the traditional bottle of champagne across the bow, as the new 362-foot-long ship slid down the ways and into the Thames River. By August, the *Nautilus* had been commissioned, and on January 17, 1955, her commanding officer, Commander Eugene P. Wilkinson, ordered all lines cast off and, with a nod to posterity, intoned, "Under way on nuclear power."

A month later, the *Nautilus*, carrying a crew of 116 men, traveled underwater from New London to San Juan, a distance of about 1,300 miles—or ten times farther than a submerged submarine had ever gone before—in eighty-four hours. In the summer of 1958, the sub made her most celebrated voyage, a top-secret run from Pearl Harbor to the North Pole, the first underwater crossing of the pole. The *Nautilus* spent her twenty-five-year active career as both a workhorse of the fleet (she participated in the Naval quarantine during the Cuban Missile Crisis in 1962) and as a show horse of U.S. technological know-how, making scores of high-visibility visits to foreign ports. After more than 2,500 dives and 500,000 miles, she was decommissioned in 1980 and designated a National Historic Landmark. Today she remains berthed in Groton, back where her long journey began, open for public viewing at the *Nautilus* Memorial and Submarine Force Library and Museum. For better or worse, it seems she has outlived the promise of a nuclear-fueled future, a promise she helped to create.

The Top-Sider

Reach into the wardrobe of Connecticut's contributions to the world of fashion and you'll find . . . not much. Oh, there might be a Stetson or a fedora made in Danbury, an old ivory comb from Essex, a wool shirt made in a Willimantic mill, but for the most part, mechanically minded Connecticut has been better at making things you can turn off and on than those you can doff and don.

In the bottom of the wardrobe, however, you may find an agreeably battered old pair of Sperry Top-Siders, complete with salt stains, unraveling stitches, unruly rawhide laces—and a pure Connecticut pedigree.

The shoe was the idea of Paul Sperry, who was born in 1895, raised in Stamford, and after an unsuccessful stint at college, became a salesman at New Haven's Pond Lily Company, a textile dying and finishing company owned by his father. While Paul dutifully put in the hours at the shop, his sustaining interests lay outdoors. He was an avid

■ Top-Sider retailers can be found at www.sperrytopsider.com. ■

hunter who spent his honeymoon shooting ducks with his bride at Chincoteague Island and a sailor who liked to race his Nova Scotia schooner, *Sirocco,* on the Sound.

It was sailing that led to the creation of the new shoe. At the time, most boaters made their way around on deck in canvas shoes with crepe rubber or rope soles. Sperry was a tinkerer at heart, registering fifteen patents in his lifetime, and he began considering ideas for a better shoe design. Such thoughts were on his mind one winter morning in 1935, when he took his cocker spaniel Prince out for a walk. After watching the dog expertly negotiate the icy terrain, he made a close examination of Prince's paw pads when they got back home and discovered tiny cracks and cuts going in all directions.

Thus—*good dog!*—the idea for the familiar crosshatched sole of the new shoe was born.

The first Sperry creation featured a canvas upper and rubber sole; the leather version, known today as the Authentic Original Top-Sider, came along in 1937 and got a big boost two years later, when the U.S. War Department chose it as one of the Navy's official shoes. After the war, following a consultation with L.L. Bean (the person, not the store), Sperry and patent-holder U.S. Rubber put the shoe into national distribution. U.S. Rubber made Top-Siders at its Naugatuck plant until 1979, when both companies were purchased by the Massachusetts-based Stride Rite Corporation, which has made them ever since. The Top-Sider stable these days includes fourteen different boat shoes for men and six for women, along with sandals, casuals, and several other lines.

The Top-Sider made the grand leap from the sailboat to the sockless feet of every self-respecting male and female preppie in America in the mid 1960s, when dress codes eased and a comfortable, presentable shoe somewhere between a traditional dress shoe and a sneaker was needed. In 1980, *The Official Preppy Handbook* anointed them along with Weejuns and white bucks, calling Top-Siders "the automatic choice with khakis." By the time Sperry died two years later at the age of eighty-seven, his creation's legacy, distinguishable even among a rising sea of imitators, was secure.

Hammonasset Beach

For some 200 years after the arrival of the first white settlers, the area of Connecticut today known as Hammonasset lay virtually untouched and unremarked upon. Shad fishermen occasionally used the uninhabited stretch of beach, and hunters went after the marsh hen there. Later there was some harvesting of the beach's other natural offerings, such as salt-marsh hay and kelp, and a shed or two went up for processing fish into fish oil.

The first permanent dwelling, a saltbox farmhouse, was built in 1828 on an island in the marsh behind the beach. The farm yielded corn, potatoes, oats, and hay, and it also raised an eyebrow or two in town, where "the beach land in Madison was for many years considered to be worthless and an unfortunate possession," according to C. Ryerson's *A Brief History of Madison*.

■ Hammonasset Beach State Park is located at exit 62 on Interstate 95 in Madison; call (860) 424–3200. ■

In 1867, however, a significant social shift occurred when the first beach house to be used solely for pleasure was erected about a mile-and-a-half west of Hammonasset. The post–Civil War industrial boom brought more leisure time to the people of Connecticut, and, as time went on, many wanted to spend their summer hours at the shore. Consequently, much of the waterfront was snapped up as private property, an ill omen for those who resided in the state's interior.

The government began acquiring land for public use in 1913, when the state Park and Forest Commission was created for that purpose. One of the first areas the commission coveted was this stretch of land in the middle of the shoreline consisting "equally of low-lying upland and salt meadows, with a mile of sandy beach equal to any in the state."

After several years of planning and negotiation, the state in 1919 paid $130,960 for seventy-five parcels of land consisting of 565 acres. The following spring, as a pavilion went up and the gates opened, the people of Connecticut began acquainting themselves with yet another long Algonquin place name.

In 1923, a local woman approached the Winchester Company in New Haven with an offer to buy 340 acres the company owned adjacent to the new park on the west. She wanted to build a resort hotel there. As it had promised, the company informed the state of the offer and gave it first crack at buying the land. But the cupboard in Hartford was bare. It looked like the land would be lost to the public, when industrialist J. Harris Whittemore, a parks commission member, put up $55,000 of his own money and agreed to buy and hold the land until the state could pay him back, which it did two years later.

Today, Hammonasset Beach State Park consists of 919 acres and is by far the state's busiest park, with nearly 900,000 visitors annually. In many ways, it serves as central Connecticut's window on the water, a place everyone can go for a swim, a hike on the beach, or just a whiff of salt air and a seaward prospect. It is taxpayers' money well spent.

Waterbury Train Tower

As a Waterbury native who has perhaps taken one too many sips of water from the horse fountain on the city green, I've long enjoyed referring to the city as the Paris of the Naugatuck Valley. In his memoirs, my father claimed that if you stood in the right spot on a certain hillside in 1948 (with a certain someone on your arm) and closed your eyes slightly, you could transform the city into Florence. In truth, however, ever since 1909, when the Union Station first opened its doors to the railroading public, Waterbury has most resembled the Tuscan hill town of Siena, in at least one major aspect.

The story actually began in 1905, when Charles S. Mellen, the president of the New York, New Haven and Hartford Railroad, took a trip to Italy with his wife. Among the places they visited was Siena, where a magnificent tower, the Torre del Mangia, dominated the town. The 335-foot-tall tower had been built in the fourteenth century to overlook the public square—the Piazza del Campo—where Il Palio, the celebrated horse race, is run for two days each summer.

■ The Waterbury train tower is located on Meadow Street in Waterbury near exit 21 of Interstate 84. ■

Upon his return to the States, Mellen firmly suggested that the next large station built by the railroad include a replica of the *torre* he had so admired overseas. He had assumed his position with the railroad two years earlier at the behest of financier J. P. Morgan, and now the two men were busy spending millions in an ultimately doomed effort to create a transportation monopoly in New England. Given their grand designs and spendthrift ways, it seemed only fitting that some of the company's major new depots be built to resemble Renaissance temples. The Waterbury assignment, quickly approved by the board of directors, was handed over to the renowned New York architectural firm of McKim, Mead and White.

In the first decade of the twentieth century, Waterbury was at the height of its great manufacturing epoch. The city's staggering production of brass and other materials created one of the busiest rail yards in the country. It was the second largest mover of freight in New England after Boston, and at one point eighty-six passenger trains arrived and departed every day. It was not uncommon to see six trains at once at the station.

In short, the railroad and Waterbury prospered together—truly helped each other get rich—and now the city would get a proper symbol of that relationship.

The new station cost $332,000. Its tower is 245 feet high, with an observation deck reachable after a climb if 318 steps. Near the top (much higher than in the Siena tower), are four clock faces designed by the Seth Thomas Company of nearby Thomaston. The dials are 16 feet in diameter, and their Roman numerals 5 feet high. Also at the top is a bell, installed in 1916, and eight gargoyles—she-wolves meant to summon up the spirit of Romulus and Remus, the legendary founders of Rome (Senus, a son of Remus, is said to have been the founder of Siena).

Since 1952, the train station and its tower have been the property of the *Waterbury Republican-American,* which has reconfigured much of the interior space to suit the needs of newspaper publishing. What once was the waiting room's vaulted ceiling now looms over the ink-stained wretches in the newsroom. The exterior, however, remains essentially unchanged as a visual feast and an astounding, indelible keepsake from one man's trip to an Italian hill town.

Hot Dogs

There is no mention of hot dogs in Shakespeare's sonnets, not a whisper in all the lines of Emily Dickinson or the books of the Bible, nothing in the "I Have a Dream" speech of Dr. Martin Luther King Jr. Likewise, "frankfurter" is not found in *Bartlett's Familiar Quotations,* nor is "wiener," "red hot," or "tube steak." Yet sometimes when I gaze upon a hot dog, I feel it deserves more poetry than I can deliver—and maybe just a squiggle of mustard.

Connecticut is a renowned pizza state (we all have our favorite) and a great place for ice cream (some say the best), but for those in the know it also ranks among the great hot dog states. Frankophiles know well our local temples of taste and will gladly make gas-guzzling side trips or even well-organized pilgrimages to visit them.

They'll head for Super Duper Weenie in Fairfield for the homemade condiments and the New Englander, loaded with bacon, sauerkraut, mustard, onion and relish; or to Glenwood Drive-In in Hamden, where the dogs are charcoal-grilled; or to Guida's in Middlefield for the buttered and grilled split-top rolls; or to Danny's Drive-In in Stratford for the volcanic chili dogs; or to the longtime Connecticut classics such as Frankie's in Waterbury, Rawley's in Fairfield, and Jimmie's at Savin Rock.

For much more on hot dogs near and far, see Jane and Michael Stern's www.roadfood.com.

There are endless discussions about the merits of various hot-dog brands (Hummel Bros. vs. Grote & Weigel, for example), cooking styles (grilled vs. boiled), rolls (traditional split-top vs. side-split), and toppings and other accompaniments. My opinion, though, is that, presuming the ingredients are fresh and of good quality, a dog is a dog. Actually, it doesn't need to be all that good to be enjoyable.

A waterlogged hot dog popped into a soggy roll and squirted with packet mustard can be delicious if the day is nice and the ballgame is good.

There are certain places in Connecticut, however, that just feel especially right for hot dog consumption, and the greatest of these may be Blackie's in Cheshire. Located on a shady bend of the road near the Cheshire-Waterbury line, Blackie's started out as a gas station and began serving hot dogs in 1928. Eventually, the food proved the better way to go, and Blackie's began to take on its present configuration.

It is one of those places that effortlessly transports you to another time in Connecticut, to a perpetual summer evening in 1954. When the two garage-type doors are up, the central counter is open to the air; on either side are small, wood-paneled dining areas. In one is a pinball machine that no one ever seems to play. On the walls are old photos of the founders, a few newspaper clips, and signs that say NO DANCING.

The menu at Blackie's is so simple that people commonly pull up to the counter and just say, "two" or "three," depending upon how many hot dogs they want. The Hummel Brothers hot dogs at Blackie's are boiled in peanut oil and then tossed onto the grill before being served in side-split rolls. They are good, but with a topping of hot-pepper relish that road-food expert Michael Stern once described as "transcendent," they are made great. There are many anecdotes about the secrecy surrounding Blackie's relish, and if you go to Blackie's you can hear the old stories buzzing like June bugs around the neon. Those are more tales you'll never read in Shakespeare, but they'll do just fine for a midsummer night in Connecticut.

The Wildcat

The 1920s were very good years for roller coasters and the thrill-a-minute guys and dolls who liked to ride them. (Indeed, for *coasteristas* it was a period matched only by the last decade or so, when dozens of ever higher, faster, and more improbable rides have gone up all over America.) Seventy-five years ago, in the midst of a decade notoriously devoted to silliness and fun, the soaring new coasters, with their giddy heights and swooping turns, stood as perfect symbols of the age. All the classic amusement parks in the Northeast raced to throw the great wooden structures into the air and christen them with scary meteorological names. At Coney Island in New York, the Thunderbolt opened in 1925, the Tornado in 1926, and the legendary Cyclone in 1927. Revere Beach near Boston built its own Cyclone to greet park goers in 1925 and opened the Lightning two years later. Formidable wooden coasters took up residence at Rye Playland, Palisades Park, and along the Jersey shore as well.

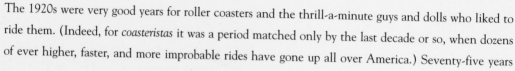

Take exit 31 off Interstate 84 to get to Lake Compounce Theme Park in Bristol, (860) 583-3300.

Closer-to-home, Savin Rock, located on Long Island Sound in West Haven, was probably the state's premier destination for summer thrills. It boasted two big coasters, both built in 1925 and both, as it turned out, pretty short-lived: the Devil, which ruled over Liberty Pier until the pier burned down in 1932, and the Thunderbolt, which operated until 1938 when it was essentially destroyed by the great hurricane of that September.

The roller-coaster craze reached central Connecticut in 1927, with the opening of the Wildcat at Lake Compounce in Bristol. The park had actually built its first roller coaster, the Green Dragon, in 1914, but by the standards of the 1920s it was deemed too tame. The big, new, double out-

and-back coaster immediately captured the public's attention and helped move Compounce, which had first opened as a picnic park in 1846, into the front ranks of New England playgrounds. Designed by Herbert Schmeck and built by Philadelphia Toboggan Coaster Inc., the Wildcat was 2,746 feet long, reached a height of 85 feet with a drop of 78 feet, and attained a speed of 48 miles an hour during an 85-second ride.

Those numbers may not count for much these days, but for years the Wildcat stood alone as Connecticut's only essential amusement-park ride. Its huge, spidery, white-painted framework domi-

nated Compounce's lakeside setting, and at night especially, the periodic rise and fall of screams and rushing cars as it went through its paces overhead were as rhythmic and as familiar a summer sound as waves advancing and retreating on the shore.

These days, the Wildcat still operates at Lake Compounce, but its primacy at the park is a thing of the past, undone by splashy water rides, a 1997 steel coaster called Zoomerang, and a brilliant 2000 wooden coaster called Boulder Dash that runs through the trees and alongside rock ledges. Still, whenever national Roller Coaster Day comes up each summer, it might be nice to ride the Wildcat once or twice and see what all the fuss was about.

The Hitchcock Chair

After tilling brutally rocky soil, boiling soap and washing clothes by hand, chopping wood for fuel, setting out traps for food, and thrashing the eight young 'uns with a hickory switch, a weary Connecticut soul in the early nineteenth century needed a good place to sit down at the end of the day.

The typical home had several pieces of furniture designed for this purpose, but none of them was especially comfortable. There was a real need in the young, growing nation for a chair that was mass-produced, well made, handsome, and priced to fit the common man's pocketbook—indeed, just the sort of chair that Lambert Hitchcock began making in his Barkhamsted factory in 1818.

Hitchcock had been born in Cheshire in 1795 and was drawn to the furniture-making business at a very young age. Up until that time, chairs were produced one at a time, with the last one made typically serving as a model for the next. Just to the south of Litchfield, however, in the Naugatuck River Valley, clockmakers such as Seth Thomas and Eli Terry had begun turning out new clocks with interchangeable parts. This allowed them to manufacture the clocks more quickly and efficiently, sell them more cheaply, and repair them far more easily. Hitchcock, barely twenty years old, saw that the same revolutionary approach could be brought to the making of chairs.

Flush with the entrepreneurial spirit that seemed to be everywhere in newly industrial Connecticut, he scoured the area and found a small, empty sawmill at the confluence of the Farmington and Still Rivers in Barkhamsted. The location struck him as a good one: The rivers would supply the water power he needed to run his machinery, and nearby forests would provide the birch, oak, and maple he wanted for his chairs.

The Hitchcock chairs of 186 years ago had characteristics we would find familiar today. Made of sturdy hardwood, they featured backs with curved tops, broad, gently curved back slats, and narrow cross pieces below. The seats were made initially of rush taken from local cattails, then cane, then plank. The chairs were painted black over undercoats of yellow, green, or, most commonly, red, with distinctive stenciling that included baskets of fruit, bunches of grapes, horns of plenty, or fountains with birds. Stenciled on the back was "L. Hitchcock, Hitchcocks-ville, Connecticut, Warranted." They sold for about $1.50 apiece.

By 1825 a big new brick factory building had taken the place of the old sawmill, and about a hundred workers were producing more than 300 chairs a week. But transportation problems, as well as a host of imitators, began to hobble the growth of the new company, and by 1829 Hitchcock was forced to declare bankruptcy. He managed to reform in 1832, but in 1848 Hitchcock severed relations with his partners, and he died insolvent and unhappy four years later—yet another visionary done in by the harsh realities of commerce in early America.

His chairs live on, however. They were produced under several different names for a decade or two following his death, then went out of production entirely until 1946, when the company was reborn on the very spot of its origin, in the section of Barkhamsted now known as Riverton. Over the last half of the twentieth century, the chair once again assumed a familiar place in American homes, often stenciled with the name and seal of a prominent college or university. Until early 2006, when it, too, went under, the modern-day Hitchcock Co. produced a line of furniture that went well beyond even the fevered imaginings of young Lambert Hitchcock—but its roots could not have been more firmly attached to the greatest days of Connecticut ingenuity.

Pepperidge Farm White

Back in 1937 there was lots of bread on Connecticut's grocery shelves, but it wasn't very good. It was white and soft, and it had the approximate taste and nutritional value of bubble wrap. But it was cheap. It cost a dime a loaf, so people bought it and ate it, even though they probably felt vaguely dissatisfied. Although most no longer baked bread themselves, they remembered what a home-baked loaf tasted like and how good it made them feel to smell it baking in the oven.

It was at this time that a Fairfield housewife named Margaret Fogarty Rudkin was searching for bread she could feed her son, who suffered from allergies. Rudkin, then thirty-nine, was the wife of a New York stockbroker. She could afford the best of care for her son but was frustrated that she couldn't find something as simple as a wholesome loaf of bread. A resourceful sort—and apparently having run out of patience—she researched what went into a good loaf of bread and began making her own.

■ Go to www.pepperidgefarm.com for more about the history of Pepperidge Farm. ■

Rudkin later recalled that those first efforts were rock-hard and inedible. Soon, however, she hit her stride and took a sample to her son's doctor for a taste. He liked it so much that he ordered some for himself and for a few of his other patients. Thus emboldened, Rudkin next brought samples to nearby grocery stores. The grocers, too, liked what they tasted but wondered if the public would pay 25 cents a loaf for it. They did. The bread, by now named Pepperidge Farm after a large Pepperidge tree (also known as sour gum) on the Rudkin property, stirred a fundamental hunger in the public. Within months, Rudkin was forced to move her baking out of her kitchen and into a backyard stable that once housed polo ponies. Soon business was so good that Pepperidge Farm had to leave the farm altogether for a larger bakery in Norwalk.

The new company prospered in the years that followed, surviving the war and a challenge from another nascent baker, Arnold, which in 1940 began producing similar premium loaves in Stamford (later Greenwich). In time, Pepperidge Farm won a place in consumers' hearts as a homey sort of company where tradition and quality counted for a lot. At first Margaret Rudkin herself appeared in advertisements, extolling the virtues of unbleached flour, honey, and eggs. Later, a laconic New England farmer named Titus Moody (played by actor Parker Fennelly) took over with great success as product spokesman.

By the time Rudkin sold Pepperidge Farm to the Campbell Soup Company in 1961 for $28 million, she was a nationally known figure and a legend in entrepreneurial circles (and certainly the spiritual godmother of another Connecticut tastemaker, Martha Stewart). The company has added many new products over the years, including cookies, soups, and every manner of Goldfish crackers, but it has never strayed far from its original calling.

In late 2001 the $600-million company announced it had at last outgrown its bakery in Norwalk, one of seven around the country, and would move—but not out of Connecticut. A huge new facility was built in Bloomfield. Loyalty to its birthplace? Maybe Pepperidge Farm *does* remember.

Heublein Tower

People have always loved a view. Standing high on a hill overlooking the surrounding countryside, especially after a brisk climb, clears the head for day-dreamy contemplation in a way that only a solitary walk on the beach or a long spell over a good map can match.

Of course many of the best views in Connecticut were long ago gobbled up by people with foresight and money. The charms of Long Island Sound, for instance, are these days usually best observed from pricey private terraces and master bedroom suites, while many of the choicest inland hillsides and ridgelines are, as they say in the restaurant business, reserved. Such is certainly the case along

■ Heublein Tower is located in Talcott Mountain State Park on Route 185 in Simsbury; call (860) 424-3200. ■

Talcott Ridge in Avon and Simsbury, where, in recent years especially, heavenly views have often been hogged by alarmingly large houses of questionable taste.

Not so along private Monte Video Road in Simsbury, however, where the few private houses are reasonably tasteful and discreet or, better yet, nearly invisible to the passer-by, and where arguably the best view in Connecticut remains open to all. This magnificent five-state vista can be found at Heublein Tower, the ultimate look-at-me country retreat built in 1914 at the high point of the ridge, some 980 feet above sea level, where it soars from the treetops like a Tyrolean castle overlooking the Rhine.

Even eighty-seven years ago, the spot had already long been in use by previous builders of towers. The first such structure was put up in 1810 by Daniel Wadsworth. It was replaced in 1867 with a 50-footer built by Matthew Bartlett and visited by Samuel Clemens and other ruck-sacking luminaries of the day. The current tower was designed and built as a very tall summer house, with living and dining rooms, bedrooms, sleeping porches, baths, kitchen, and servants' quarters. It rises 165 feet above the ridge and was the property of Gilbert F. Heublein, who, with his brother Louis, had taken the family hotel and saloon business in Hartford and turned it into a successful international purveyor of food and liquor.

The Heublein family sold the tower in the 1940s to the *Hartford Times*. It is said that, while visiting the tower in 1952, Gen. Dwight D. Eisenhower received the word that he would be the Republican Party's nominee for president. The tower next fell into the hands of a group of developers, whose grand plans for an inn and restaurant at the site were thoroughly dashed by the neighbors. In 1966 the state bought the tower and surrounding acreage, made it part of Talcott Mountain State Park, and in its uniquely unseeing way, nearly destroyed the building while bringing it up to code.

These days, a small band of partisans, the Friends of Heublein Tower, are painstakingly attempting to restore the tower to its former glory. They are tracking down original furniture, fabrics, and place settings and soliciting carpenters, electricians, and others who might lend a hand. The group is undermanned and underfunded, but the view and the building that provides it seem well worth it. "If you want the building to come alive again," said Friend Kathy Hoidge, "you've got to hang in and work on it."

Raggedy Ann

In a world rife with suspect redheads and little girls' dolls designed to look like jailbait, Raggedy Ann shines through like a visitor from a more benign sphere.

With her simple, cheerful features and her "I Love You" heart, she'd probably never pass an audition before the marketing hot shots at a modern-day toy company. But her survival skills are impressive. She weathered all the ups and downs of the twentieth century with nary a scratch (although her hair did seem

■ To learn about Raggedy Ann exhibits and events, call the Norwalk Museum at (203) 866-0202. ■

to grow redder with each passing decade). She's successfully fended off the likes of Chatty Cathy, Betsy Wetsy, Cabbage Patch Kids, and Barbie. You'd certainly never guess she was more than ninety years old.

Raggedy Ann is a Connecticut girl. Her creator, Johnny Gruelle, came to New Canaan in 1910 to pursue freelance opportunities as an illustrator and cartoonist. His studio overlooked the Silvermine River. "It is the most delightful spot one could find anywhere," he wrote to his friends back home. "I am sure that there is nothing in Ohio or Indiana which can begin to compare with the ideal situation we have here. There are artists, sculptors and illustrators of international reputation."

Within a year he was producing a full-page Sunday comic called "Mr. Twee Deedle" for the *New York Herald* and raising his family in the Connecticut countryside.

The idea of a little rag doll was something Gruelle mulled over for nearly ten years before Raggedy Ann was born. According to his wife, Myrtle, he most likely discovered the prototype in his parents' attic.

"While he was rummaging around, he found an old rag doll his mother had made for his sister," she recalled. "He said then that the doll would make a good story."

After that, a familiar figure began popping up regularly in his drawings and doodlings. For example, one of the characters in "Mr. Twee Deedle" was never without her floppy, yarn-haired companion—later called "an unmistakable forebear of Raggedy Ann."

The idea finally came to fruition in 1915, when Gruelle obtained a design patent for the doll, registered a trademark for the name and logo "Raggedy Ann," and with his family's help, began making and selling a small number of handcrafted dolls as true Connecticut products. In 1918 the P.F. Volland Company of Chicago published Gruelle's *Raggedy Ann Stories* and began manufacturing the dolls on a far larger scale. As more books came along and many more dolls were produced (Raggedy Andy joined the party in 1920), the little redhead became one of the most highly recognized faces in the world.

Raggedy Ann & Andy remain popular today. The dolls are produced by at least three companies—Hasbro, Playskool, and Dakin—in many different sizes and configurations. At last check, there more than 2,000 Raggedy Ann-related items listed on eBay, where both vintage and new dolls sell briskly. A visit to the online Raggedy Land Gift Shop turned up an impressive number of items, including Raggedy Ann & Andy figurines, rubber stamps, and outfits for every month of the year.

If you'd rather pay homage to Raggedy Ann in person, you can do so at the Norwalk Museum in South Norwalk, which houses a small permanent exhibit. She may be another native who's moved on to bigger things, but she'll always be welcome back in our arms.

American Shad

Every year a million or so sexed-up American shad celebrate spring break by returning from the ocean to their freshwater birthplace in the Connecticut River. Beneath a yellow spring moon, the shad meet and greet and splash and spawn 'til dawn, in a reasonable imitation of what vacationing college students do every year in Panama City Beach and South Padre Island. The shad run is a ritual that courses through Connecticut's history like . . . well, like the river itself.

In the state's agrarian days, before the architects of the industrial revolution built dams across the Connecticut that made spawning runs impossible, shad were astonishingly numerous during their April-to-mid June frenzy. Such was the abundance that special fishing companies were organized for the ten-week period, and most of the catch was salted, packed in barrels, and sent down the river to New York, Philadelphia, Baltimore, and as far away as the West Indies. Some of the fish were consumed locally, but shad was derisively known as "poor man's salmon," and it was never something that people seemed to enjoy eating. Farmhands working in the river valley towns even demanded that a limit be placed on the number of times they could be fed shad. Excess fish were often used as fertilizer.

■ The Haddam Shad Museum, in Higganum at 212 Saybrook Road, is open by appointment; call (860) 267-0388. ■

In one account published in 1859, an old-timer recalled, "In the last century, hundreds of people came in the spring to fish for salmon and shad, some say 1,500 men at once, carrying away bags of the fish on horseback. The shad were so plentiful that they were often thrown back into the water as worthless. It was considered disreputable to eat them, indicating poverty. Mr. Judd tells of a family that being surprised at dinner hid the shad under the table."

Today, in these days of a global fish market with Chilean sea bass, orange roughy, Dover sole, and yellow fin tuna, shad still doesn't find much favor on the menus of Connecticut restaurants. "Fifteen or twenty years ago, shad was requested more," said Tom Fernandez, a long-time restaurant chef with many year's experience cooking Connecticut foods, "but it's an oily fish; either you love it or hate it. It can be a hard sell when you can get all these other fish that people naturally enjoy more, fresh, from all over the world."

Nevertheless, in certain communities along the Connecticut River, the spring shad run remains a cause—or an excuse—for celebration, and an iconic throwback to colonial days. Annual shad bakes and related activities are held in Essex, Windsor, and Old Saybrook. There's even a shad museum in Haddam that's open on Sunday afternoons during the run (mid-April through the end of June). If you want a truly authentic Connecticut experience, head for Spencer's Shad Shack, also in Haddam and one of the last left in the state, where freshly boned fillets and shad roe are sold in season. They say that to cook them the way the pros do, place the fillets on planks made of aged oak and bake over an open fire—but open a can of tuna just in case.

Steamed Cheeseburger

For a state that's been around for as long as it has, Connecticut hasn't done a very good job of producing or marketing signature native foods or dishes. Go to the grocery store and you'll find Vermont and New York cheddar, but no Connecticut cheddar. Go out to eat and you can order Boston cream pie, Buffalo wings, or Philly cheese steak, but not Hartford fries or Cornwall apple crisp.

Even the dishes that could be considered native to the state don't wear Connecticut name tags. When the hamburger sandwich was created at Louis' Lunch in new Haven nearly a hundred years ago, why on earth did they decide to name it after a city in Germany? Just imagine for a moment a world plastered with McDonald's signs declaring: "Over 100 Billion Newhaveners Sold." Similarly, when the first hot lobster roll was served along the shore—very unlike the cold lobster salad found elsewhere—couldn't whoever was in charge have put it on the menu as a Noank roll or Seaside Park sandwich? The same goes for the white clam pizza. Why not call it a Wooster white pie, after the New Haven neighborhood of its birth?

■ Get your steamed cheeseburger at Ted's, 1046 Broad Street, Meriden, (203) 237-6660. ■

All of which brings us to the steamed cheeseburger, perhaps the most peculiar and iconic Connecticut dish of all. "In our thirty years of traveling we have never seen one outside Connecticut, in fact never seen one outside of central Connecticut," said Michael Stern. Stern and his wife, Jane, are the nation's leading experts on native and roadside foods and longtime Connecticut residents.

It is said that the steamed cheeseburger was first sold off the back of a mobile lunch cart in Middletown in the 1920s and later became an indoor feature at restaurants, mostly in Middletown and Meriden. It is still served in several spots in the area, including O'Rourke's Diner in Middletown and the Lunch Box in Meriden, but the high altar of the steamed cheeseburger is a little place on Broad Street in Meriden called Ted's. At Ted's, the cheeseburger is the only food on the menu. Here you'll find the authentic steam cabinets with their rows of compartments into which proprietor Paul Duberek alternately places the ground beef and hunks of Vermont cheddar cheese. When both are thoroughly cooked, he places the beef on a hard roll, ladles the melted cheese over it, adds lettuce and tomato if you wish, and slides the combination across the counter.

Duberek says he sells about 200 burgers a day. Business is steady, he adds, and as long as he can keep his steam cabinets in good working order, he's confident that devotees of this unique treat will continue to find him. It's a good thing, too—these Connecticut foods need a nice place to call home.

Barn Red

November is the time of year when barns re-establish their presence in the Connecticut countryside. The riot of fall color has quieted, the tree branches are bare, the fields have turned to brown and dull gold, and suddenly that most humble and hardworking of our native buildings becomes visible once again.

There are all sorts of barns in Connecticut. Once used for horses and carriages, city barns, if they're still standing, are used mostly for cars. Tobacco barns, usually called sheds, are still employed in the Connecticut River Valley north of Hartford. And barns have been built in recent years strictly for show, usually as appendages to splashy country estates and to house things like squash courts and private microbreweries.

There are also the true working barns, some long abandoned but many others still very much on the job. These barns come in all sorts of permutations, usually rectangular but sometimes round and even octagonal. There are cavernous dairy barns and standard two-or-three-bay Yankee barns entered through a single double door. Indeed, the barns in rural Connecticut and New England can come in almost any shape or size, but they are almost always the same color: red. Over the years the red-painted barn has become as much a part of our collective consciousness as the white-steepled church or the war cannon on the town green. But Connecticut barns didn't begin with red paint; they sort of grew into it.

According to the late Eric Sloane, the author, artist, Kent resident, and expert on most things associated with rural America, the first red paint on barns appeared in the early nineteenth century in Pennsylvania, where German farmers sought to make their buildings more cheerful and attractive. Apparently, their dour New England counterparts believed it was ostentatious and expensive to use paint on any buildings, and they professed to enjoy the patina of raw wood siding both on their barns and homes. In addition, highly religious farmers such as the Shakers regarded bright colors or virtually any color at all as sinful.

The Pennsylvania barns on which color first appeared were made mostly of stone, with only the south sides containing wood, so they didn't present great opportunities for paint sales. In New England, however, the barns were made completely of wood, and all four sides could be painted, so that's where the

paint salesmen began to concentrate their efforts. By 1850 or so, the paint makers had come up with the pitch that paint preserves wood. Even frugal Yankees began to paint their houses and barns, and, for the latter, red quickly became the color of choice. According to thebarnjournal.org, red was used mainly because it was cheap, using ferric oxide—rust—as a prime ingredient, along with resin and linseed oil. The fact that dark red collects heat made it a smart choice for Connecticut winters, too, although not much fun in summer.

Of course some farmers were so thrifty that they didn't want to buy their paint at all, at any price. Sloane relates a story that the earliest red paint was made of animal blood and milk; this concoction did exist, he said, but it was used mostly for wooden boxes or furniture. Because old blood darkens rather than stays red, the homemade paint turned out more brown than red.

According to one present-day Connecticut farmer, finding the proper red paint for the barn became a problem recently when lead-based paints were phased out. Most of the replacements had a tendency to fade to a purplish-pink color that fell far short of the original. But now, he says, Benjamin Moore has come to the rescue with its "Cottage Red"—a rich, evocative hue, and well worth a price that must have those old Yankee farmers spinning in their graves.

Yale Bowl

With the possible exception of its famous come-from-behind tie in 1968 ("Harvard beats Yale 29–29," the *Crimson* headline famously read), no football game in Harvard's epic rivalry with Yale could have been more satisfying than the one that took place on November 21, 1914, the day the new Yale Bowl opened.

The first game in what was then the largest stadium in America was a spectacular athletic and social event, a front-page story throughout Connecticut and the entire Northeast. Between 10:15 A.M. and 1:15 P.M. on the day of the game, special trains loaded with fans arrived every four minutes at the New Haven depot—twenty-one trains in all from New York, fourteen from Boston, six from Springfield—and from there the journey continued via open trolley cars out to the Bowl, with students joining in along the way. In addition, more than 7,000 "machines," as cars were commonly called at the time, made the bumpy trip to park and presumably tailgate on the grassy playing fields surrounding the new coliseum.

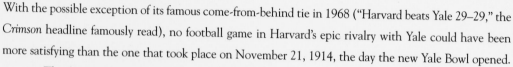

■ Yale Bowl is located on Route 34 in New Haven. Get a Yale football schedule by calling (203) 432-1400. ■

Following the game, the big party continued. All hotels and restaurants in the area were completely booked. One newspaper reported that a local hotel's dance floor that night "attracted many enthusiastic artists of the latest trots and hesitations," and that at one point all the revelers in the dining rooms and ballroom alike stood and sang "It's a Long Way to Tipperary," with the band struggling to keep up with the many encores.

As for the game itself, the throng of more than 70,000 witnessed a stunning 36–0 triumph for Harvard, an unexpected drubbing that prompted the *New York Times* to intone gravely, "In the dusty archives of Yale's proud football history, there is no account of a blow as severe as this."

In the many years since that day, the fortunes of the Yale Bowl and the team that plays there have risen and fallen any number of times. No day could compare with October 22, 1921, when fearsome Army came to New Haven to play its first non-Navy game away from West Point and, before a crowd of 74,000, fell to Yale, 14–7. Or October 26, 1929, three days before the Crash, when Albie Booth called the plays, returned kicks, punted, kicked the extra points, scored three touchdowns, and led Yale once again over Army, 21–13. And over time the Bulldogs took their revenge on Harvard, holding a 64-48-8 advantage in the rivalry at last check.

Yale Bowl has hosted other events over the years, including rock concerts with the Grateful Dead and Led Zeppelin, the 1995 Special Olympic World Games, and two seasons of New York Giants pro football in 1973–1974 while Yankee Stadium was being renovated. But the football days of national headlines are long gone. The Saturdays of playing Notre Dame or even UConn gave way years ago to playing the likes of William and Mary—and these days Yale might have trouble beating Peter, Paul, and Mary.

Still the ancient pitch remains, and when Harvard comes to play little else matters. Alumns and purists come out, hoping for a chilly day under a steel-gray sky, something warming in hand, and brilliant moves on the field—a flashing halfback, a sudden turn of fortune—to make us rise from our seats. The crowd roars. The Bowl lives.

Eastern Oyster

It no doubt took a lot of nerve to be the first person to pry open an oyster and eat what was inside. Once the initial deed was done, however, the rough-hewn mollusk grew to become a Connecticut staple, and a source of considerable local pride and profit. Whenever September arrives and the oysters once again begin to fatten in their shells following the rigors of the spawning season, it reminds us that the Long Island Sound may be our most spectacular icon of all—and calls to mind a few key things to know about our official state shellfish:

☐ Try the oysters at the Norwalk Oyster Festival, held every September; call (203) 838-9444. ☐

☐ Native Americans pulled oysters from tidal rivers and coastal embankments as early as 4,000 years ago and consumed them to supplement their diet, which was mostly meat and vegetables. The European colonists later used the shells for fertilizer and even for paving roads. By the mid-1800s, the oyster industry was firmly established in Connecticut, as the bivalve became a fashionable item at the American table and no banquet menu of the day was complete without it.

☐ Despite all the fancy place-of-origin names for oysters you find these days on restaurant menus (Duck Island, Spinney Creek, Rumstick Point, Moonstone, Watch Hill), all the oysters that are harvested from Florida to Nova Scotia are essentially the same. Those from the Sound are usually called Blue Points, after an old Long Island oystering village.

☐ In Long Island Sound, spawning takes place during May, June, July, and August. Of the 60 million eggs that an adult female oyster may produce in the wild each year, only 42,000 survive the larval stage to settle on the sea bottom, and of those a mere 13 make it through the three or four years to adulthood.

■ Protein makes up about 50 percent of the oyster meat, carbohydrates 25 percent, and lipids less than 20 percent. Oysters are low in saturated fat and a good source of omega-3 fatty acids, recommended to prevent heart disease. Consuming a half-dozen a day will supply your daily requirements for iron, copper, iodine, magnesium, calcium, zinc, manganese, and phosphorus.

■ Oysters can hear. According to the nineteenth-century bivalve authority Professor John A. Ryder, "One can not noisily approach an oyster bank where oysters are feeding without their hearing so that instantly every shell is closed."

■ The oyster's diet seems impressively New Age, consisting mostly of diatoms, rhizopods, infusoria of all kinds, monads, spores of algae, and pollen grains blown from trees and plants on shore. The food is drawn into the gills with sea water (about four gallons per hour), but while the water goes right back out again, the food slides into the oyster's mouth.

■ Oysters count among their enemies—other than humans—the drumfish, various skates and rays, the drill (a snail-like mollusk that with its rasping tongue drills into the shell of the immature oyster and eats the soft parts), the boring sponge (which consumes the shell), and the starfish, a particular scourge in the Sound, where, according to one observer, "vast swarms sweep across the beds, devouring all oysters in their path."

Unfortunately, another enemy, MSX disease, has decimated Connecticut's oyster-farming industry since it first struck in 1997. The yield of nearly 900,000 bushels in 1993 dropped to fewer than 25,000 by 2004, although state shellfish pathologists have been hard at work on a disease-resistant strain.

Finally, there's the legend that oysters eaten in great quantity can be a powerful aphrodisiac. Many dismiss this as an old wives tale, to which we reply: Who would know better than an old wife?

Stone Walls

If you ever doubt the continuing presence of old stone walls in Connecticut, I suggest you take a November flight out of Bradley Airport, sit by a window, and look straight down into the woods as the plane becomes airborne. Without the summer's thick green canopy blocking your view of the ground, you will see in the hills the underlying patterns of ancient pastures and boundaries as defined by straight gray lines of stone.

Most of us probably have a favorite stone wall. Some are humble and falling down, while others are grand and seem impervious to time. Mine is definitely of the latter variety. This is its story.

The men came from Pontelandolfo, Italy; Krakow, Poland; and Toulouse, France, and they ended up working together in a field in Middlebury. There they labored for 5 cents an hour at the Whittemore Farm and built a stone wall that would last forever.

The year was 1907. The men lived simple lives by our standards, and they worked very hard. Most ate and slept in a wooden dormitory down by the edge of Lake Quassapaug, and they all put in ten hours a day on the farm. In the summer, they tended to the fields of alfalfa, timothy grass, and corn. In winter, they chopped wood and cut ice from the lake with a plow. In the spring and fall, once the sowing and harvesting were done, they cleared the fields and built the wall.

■ Find all you'll ever need to know about stone walls at www.stonewall.uconn.edu. ■

Much changed as the years passed. Some of the laborers drifted away to other opportunities, but many settled in the area. Of course, none is left alive now. The nature of the farm is much changed, too, since 1907. No one chops wood or cuts ice anymore, and only a few workers remain to tend the fields and make hay in summer. The sheep and cattle have disappeared from the pastures.

But the wall remains. It stands as a testament to the anonymous men who built it. It winds for three and a half miles along Tranquility Road and Whittemore Road and Route 64. It shoots up hills on to private property and down winding lanes.

The late Louis Pavan knew all about the wall and the men who built it. He came to Middlebury in 1925, after leaving his home in Northern Italy. He went to work as a laborer in the complex of fields and properties held within the wall, and he never left.

According to Pavan, it took about forty-five men eight years to build the wall. The several masons who were hired for the job were "all Italians who came from across." The laborers and masons built the wall as they went, clearing rocks from the fields and hauling them out behind teams of oxen.

"The wall goes 6 feet underground," Pavan pointed out as we rode along it, "and at the bottom it's 6 feet wide. That's a real wall. Nothing will ever happen to it. You look at it, and you know it was built back when people worked—not like now."

It is worthwhile to take a drive by the wall on an autumn afternoon when the leaves have fallen and there's a feeling of mortality in the air. The stone walls have lessons for us. They serve as reminders of our ancestors' unceasing industry and yearning for order and of their lonely backbreaking labor in every sort of weather to carve sense and sustenance from the wilderness.

And occasionally, as with the Middlebury stone wall, hard work merges with art, and a proper memorial is born.

PEZ

It's safe to say that almost no one would buy and eat PEZ candy if it weren't for the dispenser. On their own, the little pellet-shaped pastel sweets are neither very attractive nor flavorful. On the grand scale of all sweet things, I put them in the same cute-but-barely-edible category as candy hearts, candy corn, and button candy. But load them into a bright plastic dispenser with a Popeye or Mickey Mouse head on top, and PEZ is transformed. It soars. It rocks. It becomes an industry phenomenon and a Connecticut-based post–World War II icon that ranks right up there with Silly Putty and the Wiffle ball.

■ Check out www.collectingpez.com. ■

Although PEZ has been manufactured in Orange since 1973, it wasn't born in Connecticut. It actually got its start in Austria in 1927, when a man named Edward Haas brought his new candy mints to the market in pocket tins (like today's Altoids) and named them after a leapfrogging version of the German word for peppermint, *Pfefferminz*. After some twenty years of moderate success, the company came up with its breakthrough concept to put its mints in unadorned, "easy, hygienic dispensers." The new delivery system was marketed to smokers, who with one easy motion could now debonairly pop a mint into their mouths without the clumsy lid opening, lozenge shuffling, and insincere sharing with friends that goes on with mints in a tin.

It wasn't until the company's keen marketing eye turned to the United States in 1952 that the focus shifted from smokers to kids, and the cartoon heads and fruity flavors began to appear. The flavors were orange, lemon, strawberry, and cherry, with cherry later replaced by grape. First in the position of honor atop the pedestal were a Robot, a Santa Claus, and a generic Nurse and Doctor—a quartet to be followed by some 300 others over the ensuing years.

You would probably not be surprised to learn that members of the Flintstone and Simpson families have had their likenesses immortalized atop PEZ dispensers, as have Daffy and Donald Duck (no relation), and Snoopy and Garfield. But have you ever seen the Maharajah PEZ, the Psychedelic Eye, or the Wounded Soldier? Have you seen the Santa with Glasses or the vintage Eerie Spectre Diabolic? Have you ever drunk PEZ Juice or tasted of the cola-flavored PEZ of Japan or the legendary chocolate PEZ of Hungary or Thailand? I thought not. Yet there are thousands of dedicated PEZ heads out there who have done all this and much more.

They gather in Internet chat rooms or at conventions. They gather on eBay, where they bid more than $100 for a vintage Stewardess or Engineer or more than $200 for a vintage Thor. They cast their ballots at pezcentral.com, voting for the characters they most would like to see on a PEZ dispenser; leading the way recently were Scooby-Doo, the Jetsons, and *South Park* characters, while further back on the list were the cast of *Gone With the Wind*, Pink Floyd, KISS, and Howard Stern.

PEZ Candy Inc. stirs the collector's pot with periodic releases of its own new or revised characters. With sales in sixty countries and more than three billion candies sold in the United States alone each year, the company can play out its lines almost endlessly across the globe, relying on word of mouth and the Internet to get the message out (PEZ does not advertise).

Still, you have to wonder just how much better they'd do if the candy tasted really good.

Connecticut Guide

Of all the books that have set out to take a comprehensive look at Connecticut, none has managed the task as clearly, richly, and entertainingly as *Connecticut: A Guide to Its Roads, Lore and People*, published in 1938 by the Federal Writers' Project.

The book was part of a New Deal program that sent 6,000 Depression-era writers fanning out across America to document everything of interest they came across, an effort the poet W. H. Auden called "one of the noblest and most absurd undertakings every attempted by a [government]." The result, aside from putting food on the tables of otherwise jobless scribes, was 320 publications, including guides to all forty-eight states.

The Connecticut guide is now available only online and at used-book stores, where copies in good condition fetch $100 or more. A delight and a revelation from cover to cover, it begins by offering brisk, informative essays on the history, geology, economy, and culture of the state, with a chapter on Connecticut churches and substantial write-ups on some of the more notable cities and towns. Endlessly entertaining are the ten tours and twenty-four side tours of the state's highways and back roads and the hundreds of little stories, legends and eccentric characters the writers uncovered as they traveled.

In Ledyard, for example, we meet the descendants of the Rogerine Quakers, a group once so opposed to the Congregational Church that in the eighteenth century "the Congregationalists were seldom able to conduct a service without an interruption by Quaker hecklers. The Quaker men stood beneath the windows making loud noises and the Quaker women often carried their spinning wheels into the church and proceeded to work in the midst of the service."

At Meriden's West Peak, we learn the story of a spectral black dog, of whom local legend says,

"If a man shall meet the Black Dog once, it shall be for joy; and if twice, it shall be for sorrow; and the third time he shall die."

In the New Fairfield woods is the site of the Perry Boney Store, "the smallest store in the world." So small it could accommodate only one customer at a time, it was presided over by "a thin little recluse with china-blue eyes who seemed to be seeing things no other eyes could ever see."

There are tales of ghost towns and old Indian lookouts, of a cable car that carried cows over the Housatonic River to graze on distant pastures, and of Jemima Wilkinson, who it was said rose from her coffin, began preaching, and eventually went off with her newfound congregation to establish the New York town of Penn Yan. There is a settlement in Southbury of embittered former officers in the Russian Imperial Army, while "along the lower slopes of Mt. Riga [in Salisbury], tucked away in shallow mountain coves, are the cabins of 'The Raggies,' a 'lost' people about whom little is known."

As the stories pile up on page after page, it's hard not to conclude that Connecticut was a quirkier, more interesting place seventy years ago, but that it still might yield hidden treasures to those of us who, with guidebook in hand, get out and take to some of the same roads today.

Travelers Tower

When the Travelers Tower was completed in 1919 in Hartford, it was the tallest building in New England and the seventh-tallest in the world. (The Woolworth Building in New York was the tallest.)

The Travelers hierarchy was understandably well pleased with what it had produced. For an investment of $3,202,514.25 (a lovely example of insurance company precision), the firm was able to provide acres of new space for a work force that had grown from 482 in 1907 to 4,200.

The Travelers Tower meant more than just office space; it created a skyline. In its size and ambition, the new building conveyed a sense of twentieth-century metropolitan bravado that Connecticut had not seen before—and a classically romantic skyscraper style that it has not seen since.

Over the span of eight decades, the tower has provided Hartford with a symbol of strength and stability. To the public it has been exciting to look at and look out from—as anyone who ventures up the twenty-seven floors to its grand observation deck will discover. There the roof over the viewing area is supported at each corner by a Doric column. Between the columns four classic Palladian arches afford superb views of Hartford and beyond.

■ The observation deck of Travelers Tower in Hartford is open from mid-May through October; call (860) 277-4208. ■

Standing among its bland neighbors in the city's modern skyline, the Travelers Tower seems otherworldly—its contours are radical by today's standards, and its aura is variable and moody, shifting with the weather or the temperament of the observer. In the fellowship of downtown office buildings, it stands resolutely alone, a stately throwback to a dim, irretrievable epoch.

From the beginning the tower projected the effect that its creator, New York architect Donn Barber, was seeking and that Travelers officers were hoping for. On the scale of lasting monuments, at 527 feet tall it was 76 feet taller than the Great Pyramid at Giza. Certainly no one approaching the building from north or south on its broad sides would ever wonder if this company was lacking in gravitas.

Yet there is grace in the tower as well. An observer standing to the east or west will see a building that assumes approximately the same proportions as a Corinthian column; that is, the ratio of its width to its height is about one to ten, almost identical to the campanile of Saint Mark's in Venice.

Although the granite exterior of the tower has changed very little over the years, the interior has been greatly altered. Gone are the enormous workrooms, replaced by modern carpeted honeycombs. Only a few corner offices retain their elegant wood wainscoting and mahogany desks; otherwise, executives must look to their full-length portable dividers to distinguish themselves from their half-walled inferiors.

But down on the second floor, a jewel-like reminder of former days does remain: the old main entrance to the building, now known as Batterson Hall, after the company's founder, James Goodwin Batterson. Here the rooms are clad in Hauteville marble and Caen stone; the broad marble handrails end in fierce rams' heads and pillars topped with marble urns; intricate brass grillwork depicts the knight in armor that for many years was the symbol of the company.

Batterson died in 1901 and thus never saw the tower. He would have been proud of its ambition and the view from the loggia. Certainly he would have been pleased to know that the tower's great bluish-white beacon has become a bright constant in the night sky, clearly visible like a rising star to pilots as far away as Providence.

Since 1919 the Travelers Tower has been overtaken by taller buildings and by wave after wave of architectural theory, but in all that time nothing has come along to surpass the impact it made on the face of Hartford.

Cornwall Bridge

Connecticut's veneration for things old and charming finds one of its high altars in a 137-year-old bridge that spans the Housatonic River between Sharon and West Cornwall. Although there are vintage covered bridges still on the job in Kent and East Hampton, the so-called Cornwall Bridge, with its rubious good looks and tales of catlike survival, is the unchallenged postcard pinup, especially in the fall.

A number of printed sources date the present bridge to 1841, but a persuasive case for 1864 is made by Cornwall historian Michael Gannett in his *Historical Guide to the West Cornwall Covered Bridge*, from which much of the material that follows was taken. Constructed largely of red spruce timbers and following a novel lattice-truss design patented by New Haven architect Ithiel Town, the then-windowless new span was declared "the best bridge on the river" by the *Litchfield Enquirer*.

■ Take Route 128 to see the covered bridge in West Cornwall. ■

Town claimed in his sales materials that because they offer protection from the weather, covered bridges "last seven or eight times as long as those not covered." Even so, the fact that Cornwall Bridge remains with us today ought to be considered miraculous, given the depredations, both natural and man-made, that have been visited upon it almost from the beginning, when a flaming wagon of hay got stuck halfway across and was pulled out just in time.

First there were the many nineteenth-century floods, made worse by hills stripped of trees for farming and fuel, that threatened but never brought down the span. A more grinding menace came from the onslaught of increasingly heavy auto and truck traffic, which by 1925 required the first overhaul of the bridge. Not long after that, the state Highway Department suggested that an entirely new concrete bridge be built, one that would route traffic above the village of West Cornwall, as had been done downriver at Cornwall Bridge. The state, for some reason, backed off its plan, but as traffic got heavier, the bridge continued to deteriorate. In 1939, an inspector wrote that "the bridge should be closed to vehicular traffic, as only the Grace of God now prevents the structure from collapse." Finally in 1945 a twenty-ton oil truck, at twice the legal weight limit, went right through the bridge's sagging floor.

At the urging of local parties, Governor Raymond Baldwin threw his support behind a complete overhaul, which the bridge received, including its first-ever coat of paint. (The initial coat was gray, meant to simulate weather-beaten timbers; the familiar New England red was not used until 1957.)

Other threats came to the bridge by way of major, hurricane-generated flooding in 1938 and 1955 and a monumental ice jam in 1961, when only dynamiting downriver kept the ice from crushing the bridge.

In 1969 when the state swooped in again with another threatening modernization scheme, local residents found a political champion in Ella Grasso, then the secretary of the state. She pushed for and got yet another complete overhaul, this time including hidden sheets of steel, completed in 1973. The bridge's continuing integrity was assured.

And so, as often seems to be the case these days, what begins as an ode to lasting beauty ends up as an unexpected salute to cosmetic surgery.

Post Road

When the first settlers from Europe arrived on these shores, they found a network of Indian trails already in place. The trails, some blazed even earlier by animal herds, invariably presented travelers with the most direct, least taxing route between two places. The settlers took to these paths immediately and stayed with them. One of the most traveled trails in what would become Connecticut ran along the coast. Because the white man's first settlements were often along the water, the Pequot Path, as this trail was called, was much used and eventually transformed into what we know as U.S. Route 1.

Today the Connecticut portion of the old road winds 120 miles or so from Pawcatuck on the Rhode Island border down to Greenwich. It's not a pretty drive, except in rare spots. The fast-food joints and shopping centers tend to overwhelm the occasional glimpse of the Sound or salt marsh or rolling field. Indeed, the press of traffic is so relentless that one often has little time to notice anything but other vehicles bearing down in the rearview mirror.

■ A fascinating Web site dealing with Route 1 and all of Connecticut's numbered highways can be found at www.kurumi.com/roads/ct. ■

Route 1 has always been a place of traffic and commerce. As the King's Highway and the Boston Post Road, its narrow contours accommodated postal couriers on horseback in the eighteenth century and stagecoaches in the nineteenth century. By the middle of the twentieth, before the turnpike was built, the road had become notoriously overcrowded. It was jammed with short-haul trucks, short-tempered commuters, interstate haulers, and all sorts of miscellaneous vehicles. The roadside became known for its commercial crassness as well. In one 16-mile stretch just this side of the New York border, there were 1,800 signs and billboards—an average of more than 112 per mile. There were also roadhouses, honky-tonks, and the early motor hotels that writer Kenneth Roberts once described as "those unsightly nests of tourist camps that huddled in the fields as though some debauched summer hotel, on the loose, had paused on a dark night and given birth."

As the road moves today from town to town along the coast, it takes on local colorations and local names. It's called Broadway in Stonington and Tresser Boulevard in Stamford and Coleman Street, Forbes Avenue, Bank Street, Barnum Avenue, and Longhill Road in between—to name but a few. The roadside offers an array broad enough to include taking a flying lesson in Madison, placing a wager on a horse in New Haven, test-driving a Maserati in Greenwich, studying the works of the American Impressionists in Old Lyme, and buying everything from emeralds to hub-

caps at various points along the way. And let's not forget doughnuts, lots of doughnuts.

If you have a good imagination, Route 1 at dusk takes on a slightly racy atmosphere. The sky turns purple, and the road becomes a river of headlights and taillights. The roadside neon is seductive. The feeling of being on a road that goes all the way to Key West is liberating. There's a sense of sharing the road, historically at least, with highwaymen, hijackers, and bootleggers. As the night deepens the shopping centers close up for the night, and the restaurants send their patrons home. Crowds surge at popular watering holes, making connections and then scattering again.

At length all grows quiet. The affairs of the state pause for rest in the endless round of days, but the road endures. With the banality of daily life written across its homely face and with the ghosts of history dancing in its dark curves, the road abides and outlasts us all.

Gillette Castle

Good taste is one of those things that Connecticut does well. Whether it's our gently rolling hills or a town green surrounded by chaste, white-painted colonials or the generally moderate views of our citizens or the tasteful cultural influence of local stalwarts from Frederick Law Olmsted to Martha Stewart, our refined sensibility is something that sets us apart from, say, whatever it was that spawned *Fear Factor*.

Exceptions do exist, of course. Anyone can find sights and sounds that offend the senses. The touchstone for bad taste in Connecticut since the day it was completed in 1919 is the castle built by William Gillette overlooking the Connecticut River in East Haddam. It is at once garish, ugly, excessive, and weird—in fact, it's such a monument to one man's eccentricity that over the years it has become an irresistible Connecticut attraction and a highlight in the state's public park system, especially after an $11.5 million refurbishing, completed in 2002.

◼ Gillette Castle State Park is located at 67 River Road, East Haddam; call (860) 526-2336. ◼

Of course in 1919 dollars Gillette spent a lot more than that to build his castle in the first place. He'd spotted the property while cruising up the Connecticut River on his yacht in 1910, shortly after announcing his semiretirement from the stage. As an actor and playwright for some thirty-five years, he had won fame and fortune chiefly for his portrayals of Sherlock Holmes. But now he was looking for a different sort of stage, one grand enough to show off his dream house.

To some extent as Gillette sailed up the river, he was coming home. He was born in Hartford in 1853, the son of Francis and Elizabeth Daggett Hooker Gillette—she a direct descendant of Hartford founder Thomas Hooker, he a prominent abolitionist and U.S. senator who with a brother-in-law bought and subdivided the hundred-acre property known as Nook Farm. As a young man William studied at Yale, Harvard, and Trinity, but his love of the theater prevailed over a more conventional career. He got his first big break on stage in New York in 1874, when Nook Farm neighbor Samuel Clemens cast him in his new play *The Gilded Age*.

Now as a great success, Gillette was coming back to Connecticut. Atop the promontory known locally as the Seventh Sister, he began building a home that for sheer flamboyance would challenge and eventually surpass the renowned Victorian manse Clemens had years earlier put up in Hartford. Modeled vaguely after the Normandy castle of Robert Le Diable, father of William the Conqueror, Gillette's new home was built to include parapets, a turret, and a tower, all encased in 4-foot-thick granite walls frosted with a spikey fieldstone-and-mortar façade. It contained twenty-four rooms, forty-seven oak interior doors (each different), disturbingly asymmetrical windows, clunky hand-carved wooden light fixtures and switches, and lots of built-in furniture. There was a secret room from which Gillette liked to spy on his guests, a 20-foot-high timber-beamed great hall, a movable dining table on tracks, and raffia wall coverings imported from Java.

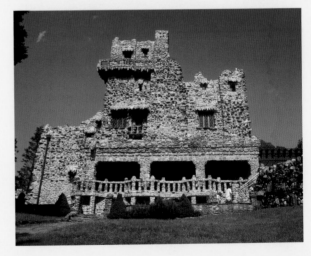

Outside, the grounds are gorgeous and the views are spectacular. Getting the most from his 184-acre spread, Gillette built a 3-mile railroad, and he enjoyed taking guests—who included the likes of Albert Einstein and Charlie Chaplin—on wild rides along the cliffs and down to the water.

Gillette died in 1937 at the age of eighty-three. In his will, he asked that his home not be sold "to some blithering saphead." The state bought it in 1943 for $30,000 and now hosts about 400,000 visitors a year—some of whom may actually think the place is quite handsome.

Silly Putty

This is a tale of two Connecticut inventions.

In 1839, New Haven native Charles Goodyear was working on ways to make a rubber product that would retain its shape and other useful characteristics under extremes of temperature. One day, he accidentally dropped a mixture of rubber gum and sulphur onto a hot stove and created just what he'd been looking for: a new substance that would eventually come to be known as vulcanized rubber.

Goodyear was a dyspeptic, half-crackpot tinker who had already experienced such poverty that he and his family had lived for a period in an abandoned factory on Staten Island, subsisting on fish he caught in the harbor. Now he would spend the remaining twenty-one years of his life trying to come up with popular uses for his amazing new find, but he had no talent for such a task. Among his misguided proposals were rubber banknotes, musical instruments, flags, clothing, and even furniture. One of his rubber desks can be seen at the Mattatuck Museum in Waterbury.

See www.sillyputty.com.

Goodyear had not an entrepreneurial bone in his body. He stood by helplessly as a succession of usurpers came along to steal or abuse his patents and put rubber to far more profitable uses. Even the billion-dollar Goodyear Tire & Rubber Company, though named after him, brought not a dime to Goodyear or his descendants. When he died in 1860 at the age of sixty, Charles Goodyear was more than $200,000 in debt.

In 1943, James Wright, an engineer in General Electric's New Haven laboratory, was working in Goodyear's long shadow. He was trying to develop a cheap synthetic rubber for the U.S. War Production Board when he happened to drop boric acid into silicone oil, and up sprang a substance that bounced higher and stretched even further than rubber—too high and too far perhaps. Although GE shared the new discovery with scientists around the world, none showed any interest in developing it. The "nutty putty," as it was called, remained a local curiosity.

In 1949, an unemployed advertising man named Peter Hodgson saw the putty demonstrated at a party (or in a toy store, as accounts differ) and liked what he saw. Although he was some $12,000 in debt at the time, he borrowed $147, bought the production rights from GE and set about packaging the substance in plastic eggs, which were then shipped in egg cartons purchased from the Connecticut Cooperative Poultry Association. He named his toy Silly Putty and marketed it to kids. After a story favorable to the new product appeared in the *New Yorker* in August 1949, the demand became such that Hodgson moved his business into a converted barn in North Branford.

By the early 1950s, the little ball of putty, which could also pick up words from newsprint, lint from sweaters, and broken glass from carpeting, had grown into a fad, right up there with baseball cards and Davey Crockett coonskin caps. Even today, as a product of Pennsylvania's Binney & Smith Inc., more than two million eggs of Silly Putty are sold every year. When he died in 1976 at the age of sixty-four, Hodgson was living in a mansion on eighty-eight acres in Madison. He left an estate of $140 million.

Now would be a good time to draw a moral or other words of wisdom from these twin scenarios, but in the final analysis it just boils down to this simple hard truth: That's the way the ball bounces.

White Clam Pizza

As I write these words and again as you read them—indeed, at any given moment in time—there are people all over the world who are thinking about, dreaming about, salivating for, or scheming over how to get their desperate little hands on a thin-crusted slice of good New Haven pizza.

Usually these poor longing souls yearn silently, but sometimes they are overcome by the need to speak out publicly and make their passion known, as when the late film critic Gene Siskel suddenly blurted out in the middle of an interview that "the best pizza in America is at Frank Pepe's in New Haven, Connecticut." Or when the likes of cartoonist Garry Trudeau or master chef Todd English similarly pledge their allegiance to the Elm City's finest.

White clam pizza can be ordered at many Connecticut restaurants, including Frank Pepe Pizzeria, 157 Wooster Street, New Haven, (203) 865-5762, and Sally's Apizza, a few doors down at 237 Wooster Street, New Haven, (203) 624-5271.

More commonly, the hungry voice is less well-known or even anonymous, rising up, for instance, from the ceaseless chatter of Internet Web sites devoted to pizza, dining out, or food in general.

"I drive from Cleveland to eat at Sally's," confesses one, referring to another revered New Haven establishment.

"Personally, I believe [Pepe's] is not only the best in America but the best on Earth, Naples included, which I have done my best to eat my way through," another announces breathlessly.

There are also those who wrongly believe that pizza, as we know it, was invented in New Haven. Although its origins are largely unrecorded (who has time to write anything down when you're so busy eating?), it seems fairly certain that pizza was first sold in this country in 1905 by Gennaro

Lombardi at the still-standing Lombardi's on Spring Street in Manhattan.

What we can claim, however, is that pizza was perfected in Connecticut. In 1925 Frank Pepe opened his restaurant on Wooster Street in New Haven and with the help of his wife, Filomena, daughters Elizabeth and Serafina, and assorted other kin, in-laws, and faithful employees, took a humble con-

struction of dough, mozzarella cheese, and tomato sauce and turned it into what is today widely thought of as a gift from the gods.

A big key to the success of Pepe's, neighboring Sally's (started up in 1938), and a handful of other top-notch purveyors is the use of a coal-fired brick oven that heats up to 650 degrees and gives the crust a scorched and blistered, but still chewy, texture. Some other important fundamentals include the use of high-quality ingredients and the liberal employment of toppings such as pepperoni, sausage, mushrooms, and the like.

While the tomato and mozzarella–based pizza may not have originated in New Haven, it seems probable that the white-clam version is a local invention to be celebrated right up there alongside the lollipop and the self-playing organ. There are enough references to "New Haven white clam pie" in pizza lore to all but nail down its Connecticut birthplace.

This pie is not for everyone, of course. Its blanket of freshly shucked clams and Parmesan cheese, sprinkle of garlic and oregano, and spritz of olive oil make for a look that would never do for a Pizza Hut TV ad.

The taste? The clamoring voices out there in the wilderness confirm its lip-smacking, life-altering deliciousness. As one exile in Texas cried out recently for all the world to hear: "You have never had a pie until you've had a New Haven white clam pie!"

The Sunfish

In 1951 a man named Carl Meinelt knelt on the floor of a boatbuilding shop in Waterbury and with his finger drew the outline of a new sailboat in the sawdust. As he did so, Meinelt's two bosses, Alexander Bryan and Cortlandt Heyniger, looked on approvingly. Five years earlier, home from the war and not wanting to return to their old jobs, boyhood friends Bryan and Heyniger had gone into the woodworking business together and named their new company Alcort, after their first names. After producing a few rowboats (the first sold to Bryan's mother for $110) and iceboats (called Skeeters), the pair had the idea of sticking a sail onto what was little more than a surfboard. They called it a Sailfish, and it revolutionized sailing.

■ For more on the Sunfish and her sister sailboats, including where you can find them sold near you, see www.teamvanguard.com. ■

Made of plywood, spruce, and mahogany, the little boat was cheap (less than $200), easily portable, blessedly simple to operate, and lots of fun. Before long, its colorful striped sails became a common sight wherever the boating crowd gathered, especially after a splashy feature appeared in *Life* in 1949 showing a fleet of Sailfish and happy, sun-drenched sailors plying the waters off Madison.

But Bryan wasn't satisfied. "I'm not sure why, but the Sailfish never really looked like a winner to me; it was too hard to sail, too tippy," he said a few years ago, sitting in his Middlebury den. "We experimented quite a bit to improve it. I knew it had to be wider, and then my wife, who was pregnant at the time, insisted that we add a cockpit."

So it was that Alcort's first employee Meinelt made his drawing in the sawdust, and a new boat, the Sunfish, was born. It met with immediate acclaim.

"If the Sailfish sold in the dozens to begin with, the Sunfish sold in the thousands," Bryan recalled. Heyniger designed the distinctive logo for the craft by tracing a circle around a nickel and adding the fins, tail, and mouth. *Sports Illustrated* called it "the simplest, best performing, least demanding and most exhilarating sailing craft of its size and price ever built." America's Cup yachtsmen Dennis Conner and Ted Turner and thousands of other kids of summer learned to sail on one. In 1977 *Fortune* named the Sunfish one of the world's twenty-five best-designed products (along with the Porsche 911 and the Trimline phone).

Today, more than 300,000 Sunfish later, the story remains a happy one. After several persuasive visits from a salesman at Naugatuck Chemical, the boat went from wood to fiberglass in 1958. It was lighter, faster, and cheaper to make, although Bryan says he missed the sweet smell of wood shavings in the shop. The company was bought by AMF in the late 1960s, and today the Sunfish, made by Rhode Island-based Vanguard, is a familiar, cheerful sight around the world. In Connecticut, it's become one of the very symbols of summer, skimming across more than fifty years of hot-weather fun.

West Rock Tunnel

In the late 1930s, as state highway engineers envisioned the majestic sweep of Connecticut's new highway system, a four-lane ribbon that would one day carry motorists from Greenwich all the way up to the Massachusetts border, their thoughts turned again and again to a sizable problem in New Haven.

The new road was supposed to be built as close as possible to the city without disturbing too many residential neighborhoods or commercial interests. The best route with the fewest curves would skirt the city's northwestern border with Woodbridge, crossing Amity Road and Whalley Avenue, and then continue on a fairly straight route to Hamden, Meriden and points beyond.

■ West Rock tunnel is located on the Wilbur Cross Parkway (Route 15), between exits 59 and 60. ■

The problem was that to get from Whalley Avenue to Hamden, the road ran smack into the 350-foot-high traprock massif known as West Rock.

Alternate routes were considered. If the road swung to the north through the so-called Bethany Gap, it would require many additional purchases of land for the right-of-way and the construction of long, expensive approaches into New Haven. A more southerly route would mean the probable destruction of existing city neighborhoods in Westville and other parts of town. Yet another possibility was to cut a route across the top of West Rock, a solution that would also require excessive right-of-way purchases, huge excavation costs, and the engineering and construction of difficult elevated approaches.

The cheapest, most direct thing to do was to build a tunnel—two tunnels as it turned out—right through the big rock. Following a long construction moratorium during World War II, that's what the state set out to do.

The twin-bore tunnels were to be 1,200 feet long, 28 feet wide, and 18.5 feet high. The new roadway would be pitched on a 3 percent grade for drainage both during construction and after the tunnel was open to traffic. To remove exhaust fumes and bring in fresh air, four ventilation shafts were run from the middle of the tunnel all the way up to a handsome little octagonal building in the woods of West Rock Park.

Work began on the project on March 10, 1948. A temporary construction plant was set up near what would become the west portals. There was a blacksmith shop, a carpenter shop, a building for general repairs, fuel tanks and pumps, and another for spare parts and supplies. A hog house, equipped with lockers, showers and toilets, was built for the workers.

The drilling, blasting, mucking, and fitting of steel ribs went on for months. It could be dangerous work. On July 1, 1948, a dynamite blast caused a rockfall that injured four men and resulted in the death of the shift boss.

The holing-through of the shafts occurred on November 8, 1948, when Governor James Shannon pulled the switch that detonated 648 pounds of dynamite for the money shot. After the requisite speeches, the official party repaired to Ceriani's Cafe in New Haven for cocktails and a holing-through dinner hosted by the contractor, L.G. DeFelice & Sons of North Haven.

When the tunnel was opened to traffic a year later, the state's wonderful new highway was at last complete. To this day, it remains the only such highway tunnel not only in Connecticut but in New England. Perhaps most importantly, as the little kids in the backseat know very well, it's the perfect length for holding your breath.

Louis' Lunch

There are those loyal cheeseheads who say the hamburger was invented in Wisconsin, when in 1891 a fifteen-year-old boy named Charlie Nagreen took the meatballs he was selling at the Outagamie County Fair and flattened them between two pieces of bread so his customers could eat them without making a mess as they strolled along the midway.

Others with a more international view make a claim on behalf of a cook in Hamburg, Germany, who toward the end of the nineteenth century came up with a sandwich consisting of a thin patty of ground beef and a fried egg enclosed between two pieces of bread. The sandwich became a favorite of sailors, who spread word of this "hamburger" as they traveled to all their ports of call.

◼ Louis' Lunch is located in downtown New Haven at 261–263 Crown Street; call (203) 562-5507. ◼

There are still other claims. In Ohio, the Menches brothers supposedly substituted ground beef for pork as they traveled the county-fair circuit, which included, of course, a stop in Hamburg, N.Y. And in Texas, a fellow named Fletch Davis served a beef patty topped with an onion slice between two pieces of his homemade toast.

All of these make very nice stories, but they share one thing in common: They're not true. How could they be, when—as all of us who live in Connecticut know—the hamburger was invented on Meadow Street in New Haven in 1900 by a man named Louis Lassen?

Lassen had opened his lunch wagon five years earlier, but according to family lore did not come up with the burger until the day a customer in a hurry needed something he could eat on the run. Lassen had been serving ground beef steaks as a regular part of his menu, but on this occasion he grabbed a hunk of ground beef, broiled it, and put it between two pieces of toasted bread. The customer was no doubt pleased as he hustled off, and Lassen had to be happy with his on-the-fly solution.

However, Lassen's initial effort drew no attention from the world at large. It might have been forgotten entirely had not Lassen and his family stayed with the original plan—for the next century.

Even with moves to George Street in 1906 and to its present location on Crown Street in 1975, Louis' Lunch has been a model for the idea of finding something you do well and sticking with it.

Indeed, the thing that sets Louis' claim of primacy apart from all the others is the fact that anyone can still go to New Haven to enjoy one of its burgers. You'll find it prepared very nearly as it was a century ago, in a setting that summons up an earlier day, right down to the generations of initials carved into the counter.

If you go during a busy time of day, you probably won't get one of the few seats, but you will be able to watch as your burger is prepared in the time-honored manner, as described on Louis' Web site:

> Each one is made from beef ground fresh each day, broiled vertically in the original cast-iron grill and served between two slices of toast. Cheese, tomato and onion are the only acceptable garnish—no true connoisseur would consider corrupting the classic taste with mustard or ketchup.

Now and always, the hamburger is the thing at Louis'. It is the ur-burger, the real deal, the original item, one of the crown jewels among all the inventions of this very inventive state. In fact, now that I think about it, I'd gladly pay you Tuesday if you'd take me to Louis' Lunch today.

Town Greens

If the ancient Egyptians believed in the mystical properties of the pyramid, it is clear that ancient New Englanders believed just as devoutly in the grassy rectangle—also known as the town green. From one end of Connecticut to the other you see them, these central greenswards with their benches and gazebos, their Civil War monuments, rippling flags, and whirling flocks of pigeons. As much as anything still in daily use, these town greens connect us with our distant past and remind us of how our communities were first laid out and organized.

In planning a new Connecticut town as they arrived in the seventeenth century, the English settlers typically first reserved the best land for farming and then found places, usually close together, for their own dwellings. Right in the middle of it all, they made a space for land they would hold in common.

According to towngreens.com, an excellent source of information on Connecticut's greens, "The central-most parcel of communal land in a town was usually reserved for the main street and/or the Congregational meetinghouse, which was the physical and psychological center of the Puritan community. While outlying common lands were used for grazing, the meetinghouse green usually functioned simultaneously as a militia parade ground, marketplace and burying ground."

Indeed, in the beginning the greens were functional but not very pretty. As sometimes happens today, people saw the common ground as a good place to sneak out to at night and dump things they no longer wanted. Reflecting a rather casual attitude toward zoning, the greens were also often built upon, with taverns, schoolhouses, and jails (sometimes with local miscreants languishing in stocks) crowding in among the gravestones.

After the Revolutionary War, as towns became more businesslike and began to take more pride in their appearance, many greens were cleared of such clutter, and town buildings and commercial establishments were pushed back to the edges. About a hundred years later, in the late nineteenth century, another big change occurred as the greens came to be viewed as important central parks in increasingly crowded cities and towns. A beautification movement swept through New England, and the greens began to take on the look we've become so familiar with.

According to towngreens.com, there are about 170 greens in Connecticut today. On many, the traditional configuration of communal icons remains practically sacrosanct. For example, the green I was most familiar with when I was growing up included shade trees and benches, a war memorial, a very tall flagpole, a permanent Christmas tree, a handsome clock, a water fountain, and several beds of tulips. There were no cannons or tanks, but there was a public-notice board and in winter signs that told you which of the city's ponds were safe for ice-skating. As I do to this day, we all have special affection for the green we grew up crisscrossing.

Some Connecticut greens are worth visiting. Lebanon's is a mile long and virtually untouched from colonial days. New Haven's is a classic urban space, surrounded by everything from historic churches to hip bistros. Litchfield's, like many others, is dominated on one end by a white-steepled Congregational church. Most of Connecticut's greens, such as Milford's, pictured above, fall into a slightly different category: taken for granted most of the time but irreplaceable.

Charles W. Morgan

As the *Charles W. Morgan* sailed out of New Bedford, Massachusetts, on September 6, 1841, for a maiden voyage that would eventually take her around Cape Horn and into the Pacific Ocean, the whaling industry in New England was reaching its frenetic peak.

The U.S. population nearly doubled between 1830 and 1850, and the expanding nation was crying out for more and more fuel for its household reading lamps and street lights. Because the oil of the whale burned brighter and longer and with less smoke than any of the alternatives, the *Morgan* and hundreds of other vessels like her were sent out to crisscross the watery globe, looking for whales to harpoon and barrels to fill—with a bloody fervor that did not begin to let up until the first petroleum well was drilled in Pennsylvania in 1859.

By the mid-1800s, whales had already been hunted by people in this part of the world for centuries. According to Robert Owen Decker's *Connecticut Whaling*, local Indians traditionally used canoes to drive whales into shallow water where they could be attacked en masse and killed. In the seventeenth century the first white settlers went after right whales that wintered in Long Island Sound, at least until the not unintelligent leviathans determined they might live longer if they spent their winters elsewhere. Beginning in the early eighteenth century, open-sea whaling became prevalent, with larger ships sailing off the New England coast to capture their prey, which they'd bring back to shore to process.

■ The *Charles W. Morgan* can be boarded year-round at Mystic Seaport. You can read all about the Seaport at www.mysticseaport.org. ■

The true heyday of the Yankee whaler began in earnest just prior to the American Revolution with the development of shipboard "try works" for extracting the oil from the blubber. With no immediate need to return to shore, whalers now could sail out into the Pacific and Indian Oceans in search of the sperm whales, whose oil was particularly fine. By the 1820s voyages commonly lasted two or three years, and a success could mean a cargo of oil and baleen (whalebone) worth more than $100,000.

In Connecticut, whaling became a key part of the economy, as support industries grew up to build and supply the 346 vessels that made their home port here. New London was by far the busiest whaling center in the state, with 260 ships making 1,000 voyages between 1718 and 1913. Stonington was home to fifty vessels and Mystic twenty-eight, but at one time or another, whalers also sailed out of Norwich, Groton, Middletown, East Haddam, Hartford, Bridgeport, New Haven, and Stamford. (It seems that Whalers was not such a far-fetched name for our pro hockey team after all.)

The *Charles W. Morgan*'s initial 1841 voyage augured well. She'd cost around $50,000 to build; three years and four months after setting out, she returned home with 2,400 barrels of oil in her hold and 10,000 pounds of baleen—all told, a prize worth more than $56,000. During the next eighty years, the *Morgan* would make another thirty-seven voyages, bringing in more than $1.4 million in profits for her various owners.

The *Morgan* returned to New Bedford in 1906, but her active whaling days were nearly over. She appeared in three movies—*Miss Petticoats* (1916), *Down to the Sea in Ships* (1922), and *Java Head* (1935)—passed through several more owners, and was finally purchased in 1941 by Mystic Seaport, where her bark-rigged profile has dominated the waterfront for more than sixty years. Following a complete overhaul in the 1970s, the *Morgan* these days takes on visitors as the last surviving wooden whaler and as a fascinating vestige of a time that has otherwise nearly slipped from view.

State Capitol

As the members of Connecticut's General Assembly filed into the state's new Capitol building for the first time in January of 1879, they must have felt proud, pleased, and greatly relieved.

I say "proud" and "pleased," because that's how politicians almost always claim to be feeling, even in circumstances when the rest of us are depressed and angry. In this case, however, the lawmakers had every right to feel genuinely happy with their new workplace, a showy $2.5 million explosion of granite, marble, and gilt set onto a prominent Hartford hilltop. They were no doubt truly pleased to have ample space for offices and committee rooms as well as lots of half-hidden Gothic alcoves perfect for buttonholing and arm-twisting. But their primary feeling would have been one of relief, because at long last the 220-year-long disagreement over which city—Hartford or New Haven—would serve as Connecticut's permanent capital had come to an end.

The "dueling capitals" problem had persisted in the state since 1665, when the union of the New Haven and Connecticut colonies was completed. At first the unusual set-up seemed to appease both sides, but as the years went by, elected officials grew tired of alternating their legislative sessions between the Old State House in Hartford and an equally old and inadequate Ithiel Town building in New Haven.

At length it was the bureaucracy that forced the issue. The growing ranks of state workers needed permanent addresses for their offices, and, in the years following the Civil War, the government agreed. But which city would get the prize?

Hartford was clearly more aggressive in making its case. In 1870 the city offered the state $500,000 toward the construction of a new building and at a public meeting two years later provided a potential site

For a tour call (860) 240-0222.

when it agreed to purchase the area that was then the Trinity College campus. There was support, too, for New Haven, but not enough. When the question was put to a statewide referendum in 1873, Hartford carried the day by a 37,000-to-31,000 vote.

As soon as that conflict was settled, another one loomed. The commission in charge of the new building chose New Yorker Richard Upjohn as the architect. The appointment of Upjohn did not sit well with powerful local businessman James Batterson, who had hoped to secure the job for himself and architect George Keller. Batterson had founded the Travelers Insurance Company in 1864 and also owned a monument company that had prospered in the wake of the war. After his bid failed, he used his considerable pull to become the contractor for the new building and along the way make Upjohn's life miserable.

According to David F. Ransom's "James G. Batterson and the New State House," the contractor repeatedly succeeded in foiling Upjohn's plans, substituted his own ideas, and ran up costs to more than triple the original estimates. For example, Upjohn's idea that the building be topped by a steeple and later by a clock tower was subverted by Batterson's strong desire for a dome.

The verdict on the final product was and still is decidedly mixed. An 1885 architect poll named it one of the Top 10 buildings in the United States. On the other hand, Frank Lloyd Wright called it the most ridiculous building he'd ever seen (probably not the only time he said that about a building).

Decide for yourself. With a lavish restoration completed in the 1980s, the Capitol's eye-popping interiors are well worth a visit. As you poke your way around the finials, crockets, and tympana, you can ponder just how things might have been different with New Haven as our capital city.

Merritt Parkway

In 1931, with the volume of traffic rising everywhere and motorists beginning to voice their anger in the voting booth, the Connecticut General Assembly authorized a new highway to take pressure off the hideously overcrowded Post Road. A "parallel Post Road" it was called, and that's what might have been built had just any governor been in power. But when Wilbur Cross signed the bill authorizing its construction, he was careful to make a distinction between a run-of-the-mill "highway" and the parkway that he envisioned. The new road, he said reassuringly, "will not be routed straight through rocks and hills and valley, like a railroad."

To begin with, the Department of Transportation decreed an unprecedented 300-foot-wide right-of-way for the road. This ensured that no billboards, roadside stands, unauthorized gas stations, or frontage subdivisions would spoil the drive. Each of the four lanes was an ample 13 feet wide, making "room enough for drivers who find it difficult to stay in their own lane." The 22-foot median strip eased the nerves of motorists who had become used to passing within inches of traffic coming in the opposite direction.

Above all, however, it was the beauty of the parkway that stood out. The Fairfield County Planning Association had the foresight to assign a beautification subcommittee to work with the parkway planners. The results of this happy marriage are evident to this day. Although the right-of-way was 300 feet, the actual road, including the shoulders, took up only about a third of that space. The remaining 200 feet was left virtually untouched. Perhaps the most extraordinary step taken by the planners was to remove small trees and shrubs that would hinder construction, transplant them elsewhere, and then bring them back and replant them in or near their original places after the pavement had been laid, along with tens of thousands of new plantings. On the day the parkway opened, the median strip was to be alive with oaks, hemlocks, maples, bayberry, mountain laurel, sweet fern, red cedar, gray birch, dogwood, and azaleas. Rarely had the words etched into Stamford's Wire Mill Road Bridge—*Qui Transtulit Sustinet* ("he who transplants, sustains")—been so appropriate.

The Merritt Parkway was named for Schuyler Merritt, a Stamford businessman and lawyer who served as a U.S. Representative from 1917 to 1937. The first section was opened on the sun-drenched morning of June 29, 1938. The official party pushed off from the state line and motored slowly over the 18-mile stretch to Norwalk, cutting a new ribbon at every town line. Taking up the rear of the official auto-cade was one Omero Catan, a New Yorker who claimed he'd also been the first nonpolitician on line at the Lincoln Tunnel, Triborough Bridge, and Eighth Avenue subway. Catan indicated to the press that he, too, was pleased with Connecticut's new road.

On the day it opened, the Merritt was amazingly pure. The roadway was concrete with little mirrors embedded in the median curb as reflectors, and there were no exit numbers, median railings, restrooms, gas stations, tolls, or commercial traffic of any kind. The astonishing bridges, each with its own little story to tell, added immeasurably to the motorist's pleasure.

Nearly seventy years later, even overburdened by traffic and menaced by drivers who insist on going much faster than the road's genteel contours safely allow, the Merritt retains much of its original beauty and tradition. The rest stops are still called canteens. The roadside signage nods back through the decades to the rustic, notched originals. On certain days, especially in the fall, under ideal and uncrowded conditions, it's a road that can carry you right back into the past.

Witch Hazel

If you take a walk through the Connecticut woods in late October or early November, you will find them lovely places to be, with a crow or two cawing from a treetop, but most of nature dormant and still. If you are lucky or know where to look, however, you will find witch hazel plants just coming into bloom, their bright yellow blossoms enlivening the otherwise monochromatic scene as if, in the words on one admiring gardener, "some whimsical party planner had, overnight, attached thousands of ruffled paper favors to the branches."

Many centuries ago, witch hazel likewise caught the attention of Native Americans, who believed that whatever special properties brought it into bloom so late in the year might also prove beneficial to humans. They steeped the twigs and leaves in boiling water and soon discovered an astringent quality that was good for healing wounds and sores, relieving aches and pains, and soothing burns and bruises. Word of these benefits was passed along to the early white settlers, who began using the liquid as a skin cleanser. (Because of the pliancy of its branches, a switch of witch hazel was also often used as a divining rod in the search for underground sources of water.)

 Find out more about Dickinson's Witch Hazel at www.witchhazel.com. ▪

The first to produce witch hazel commercially was Dr. Alvin F. Whittemore, a pharmacist in Essex, who in the mid-nineteenth century added alcohol to the brew and called it Hawes Extract, after an old Indian missionary who had earlier studied the plant's benefits. The alcohol, amounting to about 14 percent of the new solution, greatly increased its shelf life and ultimately turned a promising sideline into a full-fledged business. By 1870, production in eastern Connecticut had been consolidated under the Rev. Thomas N. Dickinson, who stepped up the harvesting of the witch hazel plants and expanded the company's mills and distilleries into Middletown, Durham, Guilford, and Higganum, while keeping the headquarters in Essex.

The product has been sold under the Dickinson name ever since. Four generations of the family guided the company to worldwide prominence, especially in the early twentieth century, and then came a sort of long, genteel decline before they sold out in 1983. Today, Dickinson Brands Inc. is based in East Hampton, where it continues to distil the witch hazel plants, which are harvested these days from other New England states as well as Connecticut, and produce products that include the original bottled extract, soaps, and even hemorrhoid pads.

Indeed, there are those who prescribe witch hazel for all sorts of maladies. Botanical.com suggests a tea made from the leaves for relief from bleeding of the stomach, complaints of the bowels, and inwardly bleeding piles. The text goes on to recommend the extract for insect bites, varicose veins, and inflammation of the eyelids and notes that the "decoction has been utilized for incipient phthisis, gleet, ophthalmia, menorrhagia and the debilitated state resulting from abortion." Another New Age purveyor, Delta Gardens, goes even further, claiming that proper employment of a "Witch Hazel Essence" ($10) "helps those struggling with dilemmas or paradox in their lives; helps one make sense of opposing ideals; and helps one integrate practical matters with ideals."

Imagine all of that—and from such a late-bloomer, too. Maybe there's hope yet for the rest of us.

Tobacco Sheds

The Connecticut River Valley is to quality tobacco what the Medoc region of Bordeaux is to fine wine. A combination of good soil, adequate rainfall and abundant sunshine has made it one of the world's premium tobacco-growing regions. Though wrapper-leaf-tobacco seed varieties developed in the valley have been planted in Costa Rica, the Dominican Republic, Honduras, Mexico, Panama and other places, no one has yet been able to duplicate the color, flavor and texture of the Connecticut Valley leaf.

What's true today, according to the above excerpt from *Cigar Aficionado* magazine, has always been true: Connecticut grows some of the most sought-after tobacco in the world. This was the case from the very beginning in 1635, when the first white settlers came to the valley and took notice of the pungent weed that was grown and smoked by the native tribes. By 1700 local tobacco was being exported back to England and the rest of Europe. A hundred years later, in 1801, the first American cigars, called "Long Nines," were being produced by a Mrs. Prout of South Windsor. By the middle of

■ The Luddy/Taylor Connecticut Valley Tobacco Museum in Windsor is a great source for Tobacco Valley information; call (860) 285-1888. ■

the nineteenth century, Connecticut leaf was used primarily for cigar wrappers, with imported tobacco used for the filler.

An observer who was traveling through the region in the late 1930s took in the rich brown fields "harrowed smooth as the chocolate frosting on a cake" and in late summer noted that "during the harvest the countryside seethes with activity, and the golden leaves, hanging in the sheds to cure, present a picture of plenty suggestive of the raiment of Ceres."

During this period, just before the ascendancy of cigarettes as the addiction of choice after World War II, tobacco farming was a major industry in Connecticut. In 1936 some 14,500 acres were under cultivation, producing more than 21 million pounds of leaf. Today, in contrast, there are about 1,200 acres devoted to the crop, mostly owned by Culbro Tobacco. Altogether, the state now grows and sells something approaching 2 million pounds of tobacco a year.

The iconic tobacco sheds were far more numerous in the Connecticut River Valley than they are today. As *Connecticut: A Guide* noted more than sixty years ago:

> Away from the road, many tobacco sheds with their red paint or weathered gray unpainted sidings seem to merge into the backdrop of distant hills. When the "vents" are open and the leaf is curing, the sheds look like many-legged prehistoric animals, standing in the rear of the fields as if guarding the fertile acreage.

The sheds are around 40 feet wide and at least 120 feet long, and they are most in use during late July and early August. The plants, having grown under gauzy white canopies all summer, are stripped of their leaves, which are brought inside to hang and cure. During the curing process, the shed is "fired," meaning the temperature is raised to over one hundred degrees through the use of burners placed on the floor beneath the leaves. Once the leaves are dry and brittle, they are bundled and then shipped off to the Dominican Republic for sorting and sizing.

Once in the smoker's hand, the Connecticut leaf takes the lead in "selling" the cigar, providing a silky, handsome look, a satisfying aroma and flavor, and a burn that is neither too fast nor too slow. Just the thing, perhaps, for a summer stroll along the shore.

Castle Craig

No doubt many have already done it, but I've always thought it would be a good challenge to find and climb all the observation towers in Connecticut. Our own haphazard travels around the state have taken us to excellent views from towers at Haystack Mountain in Norfolk, Mount Tom in Litchfield, Sleeping Giant in Hamden, Talcott Mountain in Simsbury, and the Pequot Museum in Mashantucket (where you take an elevator rather than climb to the top), and to one very marginal view from the tower in Southford Falls State Park in Southbury.

■ Castle Craig is located in Hubbard Park, 1800 West Main Street, Meriden; (203) 630-4259. ■

For our money, the best observation tower in the state is Castle Craig, which sits atop East Peak in Meriden. It is a superior tower for several reasons. First, it has a turreted top. This makes it easy for archers or riflemen to array themselves around the edge and fire down upon whatever invaders are trying to overrun the position and seize power in Meriden. Second, it commands its lofty perch as no other tower in the state. I remember seeing it as a child from the road far below and thinking it was a real castle, where the king or at least Governor Ribicoff lived a life of majesty and ease, surrounded by wizards, handmaidens, jesters, and mastiffs. Third, the view is truly sublime, looking out over much of central Connecticut and south to Sleeping Giant, New Haven, and on a very clear day, Long Island Sound.

According to Meriden's municipal Web site, Castle Craig was dedicated on October 29, 1900, as a gift from local manufacturer Walter Hubbard, who also donated much of the land for Hubbard Park, the 1,800-acre property that surrounds the 32-foot tower. There appears to be some question and even dispute concerning the model for the tower's design. The Web-site history mentions three long-debated possibilities: "Some say Walter Hubbard, a world traveler, was inspired by a Norman French tower; others by a 12-century Turkish tower on the Danube; still others maintain that it was patterned upon an ancient fortification in Craigelachie, Scotland."

The dedication ceremony was witnessed by several hundred citizens, most of whom had taken trolleys from the center of town and then made the long climb up to the tower as others rode to the top in their own carriages. For their efforts, they were rewarded with long late-autumn views, lengthy speeches, a flag-raising, and an oyster and clam roast, with old man Hubbard himself providing the many barrels of bivalves.

At 976 feet above sea level, the peak upon which Castle Craig sits is the highest spot within 25 miles of the Atlantic coastline between Cadillac Mountain, Maine, and Key West, Florida. East Peak is part of a larger traprock formation known as the Hanging Hills, which in turn is part of the Metacomet Ridge that runs from central Massachusetts straight south nearly to the Connecticut shore.

The ridge top is a lovely place to be early on a summer morning. From far below come the faint sounds of commerce and the hum of the highway as the state awakens to another busy day. Up here, though, as the rising sun warms the castle walls, the feeling is lordly and serene, at peace with the world. It must have been awfully good to be the King of Connecticut.

Lighthouses

Who among us doesn't love a lighthouse? Who isn't drawn to the image of the faithful, unwavering light flashing high above the crashing waves or through a gathering mist? Who at some point hasn't paused on a summer night to watch the sweep of a distant light and felt a pang of the deepest loneliness—and an urge to ship out to whatever exotic port the tides and time might offer?

Because of their association with an earlier day and with the romance and danger of a life at sea, each of Connecticut's twenty-one remaining lighthouses in its own way stands as an icon.

■ Some Connecticut lighthouses are open to the public; go to www.lighthouse.cc/ct.html for details. ■

Even so, the distinctive looks and personalities of some of them are particularly noteworthy. There are, for example, the lights perched atop substantial Victorian-era dwellings made of native stone at Stonington Harbor, Sheffield Island in Norwalk, and Great Captain Island in Greenwich. Another interesting trio are the chaste white towers at Lighthouse Point in New Haven, Lynde Point in Old Saybrook, and the New London Harbor. Then there's the one-of-a-kind brick and Mansard-roofed light at New London Ledge. It was designed to be in keeping with the ship captains' mansions that lined the nearby shore and was so well-constructed that it survived hurricanes and storms in better shape than some of the mansions did.

Perhaps the most familiar lighthouse in Connecticut is the smallish cylinder at Saybrook Breakwater that also graces the state's "Preserve the Sound" license plates. According to a history found at www.lighthouses.cc (an excellent source for information on all Connecticut lighthouses), the light, popularly known as the Outer Light, first went into business by the confluence of the Connecticut

River and Long Island Sound on June 15, 1886. The 49-foot-high cast-iron tower contains a basement, four main floors, a watch room, and a lantern room. For years, the light was manned by a single keeper, and the turnover rate was high. The currents of the river made it difficult to row back and forth to shore, and walking along the half-mile stone breakwater could be treacherous, especially in winter. The assignment was made a little easier and less solitary house with the appointment of an assistant light-house keeper in 1917.

The light's most severe test came on September 21, 1938, when keeper Sidney Gross and his assistant had to battle through the most powerful storm in New England history. As the intensity of the hurricane increased on that afternoon, the small bridge that connected the lighthouse to the breakwater was swept away, along with the rowboat and two large tanks of kerosene. That evening,

Gross disconnected the electric light and put an old oil lamp back into use. He stayed in the lantern room all night to make sure the lamp stayed lit throughout the storm. In the morning, he wrote in his log, "Everything swept away by hurricane except the tower."

The light was automated in 1959. Today it flashes a green light as a navigational aid, showing the way out into the great big world—and safely back home again.

We've Got Connecticut Covered